Glasgow's
Commonwealth Games

Glasgow's Commonwealth Games:

behind the scenes

Robert Rogerson

FREIGHT BOOKS

First published 2015

Freight Books
49-53 Virginia Street
Glasgow, G1 1TS
www.freightbooks.co.uk

A CIP catalogue reference for this book is available from the British Library

ISBN 978-1-910449-43-1

Typeset by Freight in Bosch
Printed and bound by Hussar Books, Poland

About the author

Born and brought up in Glasgow, Robert Rogerson is an academic geographer at the University of Strathclyde where he is deputy director of the Institute for Future Cities.

For the last four years he has been seconded to work with Glasgow City Council, Glasgow Life, and a partnership involving the city's three universities to help coordinate the research and evaluation of legacies from the Glasgow Commonwealth Games. He has assisted both the City Council and Scottish Government on the research and evaluation of legacy. Through his contact with many of the agencies and organisations involved in delivering the XX Commonwealth Games, he has had the opportunity to see first-hand the preparation and planning which led to the 'best Games ever'. As a keen competing athlete and running coach, he also brings an insight into the ways sport, communities, and cities intersect: the very essence of the Games.

Acknowledgements

Other books may be written about the 2014 Commonwealth Games in Glasgow, celebrating the 12 days when the Games were held in the city, and telling of the delivery of the Games themselves.

The different outlook of this book reflects the willingness of many people involved across the City Council, Glasgow Life, and other agencies in the city, as well as those involved with transport planning, security, and the Organising Committee (OC), to contribute their experiences. In addition, many of those involved in the earlier stages of planning, the bidding process, and in key areas of the Commonwealth Games Scotland and Scottish Government have added a wider perspective to this book. I am grateful to every one of them for their contributions and above all to the editorial board from Glasgow City Council and Glasgow Life for their valuable input to ensuring that the story here is indeed 'the inside story'. The views expressed here remain, however, those of the author.

And I am grateful for the opportunity to have been involved with the Glasgow Commonwealth Games Legacy Partnership and, in a small way, to have been able to contribute to one of Glasgow's successes. It has for me, like the city, been a privilege to be part of it, and filled with so many highlights which are unlikely to be matched again.

I hope that in reading this book you will get a feel for the effort needed to prepare the city for the Games. If you were also part of Glasgow's Games, you will have the opportunity to reminisce about the experience, find new insights into the events in July and early August 2014, and appreciate the considerable effort – and occasional disagreements – which come with planning such a major sporting event. And, if you missed out on the chance, then this book will help to explain why so many people experienced a unique buzz in Glasgow last summer and left with vivid memories of how sport and culture can unite across political and social boundaries.

Robert Rogerson

For 12 days in mid 2014, the city of Glasgow basked in some of the hottest temperatures of the year, the greatest media attention it has ever received, and in the accolade of being the host city for the XX Commonwealth Games. Across the city, sporting events and a wide range of international cultural acts and festivities made for a special, unique occasion that was truly embraced by Glaswegians and the tens of thousands of visitors who flocked to the Games and the city from around the world.

Introduction

For 12 days in mid 2014, the city of Glasgow basked in some of the hottest temperatures of the year, the greatest media attention it has ever received, and in the accolade of being the host city for the XX Commonwealth Games. Across the city, sporting events and a wide range of international cultural acts and festivities made for a special, unique occasion that was truly embraced by Glaswegians and the tens of thousands of visitors who flocked to the Games and the city from around the world. With the city nearly doubling its population over the first weekend, there was a sense that this was a special moment for Glasgow; a summer not to be forgotten.

This book captures some of these moments, recalling the highlights in sport and culture, providing not only a photographic record of the successful Games but also behind the images and headlines that represented the Glasgow 2014 Commonwealth Games. The quality of the sporting performances, the positive spectator and visitor experiences of Glasgow, and the legacies which have already been associated with the Games have all helped to make the 2014 Commonwealth Games in Glasgow a great success. And, in part, this book is a celebration of that success, offering insights into how it was achieved.

It is also an acknowledgement that success was, for the main partners involved in the Games, much more than this. The key questions this book addresses delve below the success of the Games as a sporting event to consider some of the challenges on the way, and how at times – thankfully, relatively few – decisions were made that not everyone felt were the right ones, which risked affecting the overall success beyond the event itself. But, most importantly, this book tells the story of the making of Glasgow's Commonwealth Games.

The Games

The Commonwealth Games are arguably the second largest multi-sport event in the world, attracting more than 4000 athletes from 71 nations and territories across the globe. Like its much larger cousin, the Olympics, the event is held on a four year cycle, with the Games overseen and managed by the Commonwealth Games Federation (CGF) on behalf of the members, the national Commonwealth Games Associations (CGAs). The CGF controls the sporting programme and selects the host cities, with invitations sent to all CGAs to bid for the right to be host. Whilst the event is much smaller than the Olympics – both in terms of the number of sports represented, and the length of the event – the Commonwealth Games attracts global audiences on television of approximately 1 billion people and the nations represented cover approximately a third of the world's population.

Did you know?
Scotland held the Commonwealth Games in 1970 and 1986 in Edinburgh. In recent years, the Games have been held in Kuala Lumpur (1998), Manchester (2002), Melbourne (2006) and Delhi (2010).

First held in Hamilton, Canada in 1930, the Games are designed to be an opportunity for athletes to enter into friendly competition – thus the title of the Friendly Games – in an atmosphere of celebration of sport, culture, and the values of the Commonwealth. While having imperial beginnings, the Games have grown steadily over the years and are a key symbol of the shared values of democracy, human rights, and the rule of law that binds the Commonwealth nations together. They form one of the major sporting events in the world – like the FIFA World Cup or the Olympics – and have thus become a significant part of the sporting calendar.

But the Games have also become a desired 'commodity' in the sense that, as well as having the honour of being host, the Games may offer potential benefits to the host city. Consequently, there has been competition for the right, with different cities from within the Commonwealth nations looking to secure the Games and gain advantage for their citizens.

Despite the rising costs of delivering the Games (the Melbourne Games in 2006 cost c.£1.5bn and the Delhi Games in 2010 cost c.£2.5bn), and the variable experience of gaining benefits from being host city, there has been competition for each of the recent Games, and the CGF members have had to vote on which city offered the best proposition. In a formal process, more rigorous for the 2014 Games than previously, each potential host city - named Candidate City - provides a detailed bid document to the CGF seven years in advance; this, along with other technical details, becomes the basis of selection (see Chapter 3).

One part of this bid document includes an explanation of why a Candidate City believes it can provide a successful Games and what benefits, or legacy, it hopes to gain from being host city. In making its bid, Glasgow highlighted the importance of the event to the city's long term plans for the future.

A milestone in modern Glasgow's journey

For the city of Glasgow, the Commonwealth Games represented a major step in its transformation and redevelopment. Not only did they provide an unique opportunity for Glasgow to showcase itself as a city to the hundreds of thousands of visitors who came to be part of the Games, but they also left an indelible mark on the physical, economic, and social landscape. For those who were involved in making the event happen, the Games were also about enabling them to help Glasgow to improve, marking a further stage in its long history of innovation and change.

Where the city had once been a great port of entry for people and produce to the UK, and a trade centre from the UK to other parts of the Commonwealth, the Games offered an opportunity to redefine Glasgow's relationship with the Commonwealth and beyond. The decline of the traditional heavy industries in the 1950s to 1970s left a major mark on Glasgow, eating at the heart of what had once been described as the 'second city of the Empire'. Physically, large areas of the city were transformed from once-vibrant centres of manufacturing into industrial wastelands. This was most evident along the riverside with the closure of shipbuilding yards and the associated wharfs and warehouses which had made the city such a major trading centre. But it was also visible in communities across the city where local businesses had, for generations, been supplying the steelworks, shipyards, and other large employers. The heart of communities, such as those in Dalmarnock and Bridgeton to the east of the city centre, and Maryhill and Springburn to the north, was lost, reducing employment opportunities for families and communities whose skills were no longer needed.

Image 1:
The Finnieston Crane,
Scottish Exhibition
and Conference Centre
and SSE Hydro

Glasgow's Commonwealth Games: behind the scenes

Like many cities around the world in similar positions of industrial decline, Glasgow struggled to find alternative forms of employment and the means to help individuals and communities struggling with long-term lack of jobs, low levels of self-esteem and often poor health. Despite investment in new public housing and in public sector initiatives, the city in the 1970s had become renowned for its economic, social and health issues – perhaps unfairly captured in 'No Mean City', the 1935 H. Kingsley Long novel of life in the Gorbals part of the city.

In the 1980s, in an attempt to reposition Glasgow economically, and in an effort to change perceptions of the city, the City Council initiated a strategy to focus on using events to assist in the regeneration of communities and the city as a whole. Through investment by the council in the development of new cultural facilities, Glasgow was one of the first post-industrial cities to develop a strategy of cultural-led regeneration, becoming a benchmark followed by others such as Liverpool and Manchester. The opening of the Burrell Collection in 1983 in Pollok Park, followed by the Scottish Exhibition and Conference Centre (SECC) on the site of the former Queen's docks on the River Clyde in 1985, assisted the city to be host to major cultural events including the Garden Festival in 1988, the City of Culture in 1990 and the Year of Architecture and Design in 1999.

Building on the success of the approach, in the last two decades, the event-led economic strategy has been expanded to include sporting events. Regular international indoor athletic events were held in the refurbished Kelvin Hall and outdoor events at the expanded Scotstoun Arena. Tollcross Swimming Centre was constructed with a 50m international pool enabling world class events to be held there alongside national training facilities, and the regional football centre at Toryglen in the south of the city was opened in 2009. Together these and other investments in community sports facilities were designed to help address social and health issues, as well as generate economic wealth for the city.

Glasgow's ambitions for the Games

For the City Council and its agencies responsible for sports and culture (Glasgow Life), for community home care services (Cordia), and for the promotion of the city as an economic and tourist destination (Glasgow City Marketing Bureau), the Commonwealth Games provided a further opportunity to support the long-term strategy of transformation in the city (discussed further in Chapter 2).

However the ambition for the Games extended beyond the city itself. There was a desire to help modernise the nature of the Games, making them more inclusive, more manageable, and more clearly connected with visible legacies for a host city and those taking part in the event. The 2014 event included the largest integrated para-sport programme of any Commonwealth Games with major investment made in ensuring the venues were accessible at Games time, and for users in future to encourage greater accessibility of sport in the city. By using the existing infrastructure created by the city's investment in sporting and cultural facilities, the overall budget for the Games was limited to £575m, with nearly 20% raised through sponsorship, ticket sales, and merchandising. As part of the celebration, Glasgow sought to integrate other cultural events into the Games period, involving people in the 'event' that had little interest in sport, and it reached out in school education and through culture to strengthen connections with the nations of the Commonwealth.

For those involved with the planning and delivery of the Games in Glasgow the ambition was thus to ensure that being host to the 2014 Games helped the city economically, provided new opportunities for communities in the city, provided an arena in which sporting endeavour could be showcased, and reinforced Glasgow's position globally as an international sporting city.

And as athletes, officials, the CGF, and many others have noted, the Games in Glasgow were a great success for the city, for Scotland, and for the Commonwealth.

Image 2:
The 'Big G',
George Square

Image 3:
Clyde, the Games'
mascot, Central Station

The Games in numbers

EXPENDITURE

- The Games were delivered within the budget of £575.6m

- The 10 main construction contracts related to the Games put £669m into the economy, with 63% of that funding going to Glasgow-based companies

- Of the 711 contracts awarded, 180 were to Glasgow companies and 304 to other Scottish companies

PARTICIPANTS

- 4,818 athletes took part – including nearly 300 para-athletes – from 71 nations and territories

- 2,258 officials accompanied the competing teams

EVENTS

- 17 sports were held including 5 para-sports events: athletics, cycling, lawn bowls, powerlifting and swimming

- 9 World records and 141 Commonwealth Games records were set during the Games

VOLUNTEERS

- 12,300 Clydesiders, including 160 Accessibility Volunteers were involved along with 1,100 Host City Volunteers, more than 3,000 volunteers in the ceremonies and 80 Recycling volunteers

ATTENDANCES

- More than 690,000 unique visitors to the Games and Festival 2014

- 1.3 million tickets sold (98% of total available)

- 25,000 tickets were given to enable disadvantaged young people from across Scotland (by the OC through Bauer Group), to young people, elderly and communities in Glasgow (by the City Council) as well as to members of the armed services through Tickets for Troops

- 5000 tickets provided by Scottish Government to contributors to legacy from the Games

COVERAGE

- 75% of all television viewers in Scotland on July 23 watched the opening ceremony

- 9.4 million people across the UK watched the opening ceremony; 7 million watched the closing ceremony

- About 1 billion watched the Games internationally on television

CULTURAL AND OTHER EVENTS

- 597,000 attended the Glasgow Green and Merchant City live zones

- 160,000 visited the BBC@the Quay

- 130,000 Clyde mascot toys were sold during the Games

- £5m raised for UNICEF to help young people across the Commonwealth

But so what?

Whilst such numbers and the associated epic moments of the Games' sporting endeavours point to one measure of the event's success, major sporting events are accompanied by other statistics and impacts which can be viewed more sceptically.

Major investment is needed. Millions of pounds are spent on infrastructure - not just sporting venues, but also housing, roads, paths, parking spaces and the other physical fabric required to accommodate thousands of spectators and athletes. And millions of pounds are also spent on the delivery of the event itself - on developing the sporting programme, supporting athletes to attend, overseeing the volunteers, preparing the venues for the event and building the organisation which delivers the event, called the Organising Committee (OC). A feature of many global events on the scale of the Commonwealth Games has been the significant budget overspend, with final costs often far exceeding the initial estimates.

The budget for the Games in Glasgow was set at £485m, with an additional £90m set aside to cover security. This cost was shared between the Scottish Government (£380m) and Glasgow City Council (£80m) with the remainder being raised by the OC. And, as audited accounts after the Games have shown, they were delivered for less than the budget!

Were the Games worth this sum of money, especially when public expenditure is being constrained and there are many other priority areas? There are, of course, many ways to look at this. On the one hand, the sum expended on the 2014 Games represents only a small fraction - some 20% - of that spent four years previously at the Delhi 2010 Commonwealth Games. In a large part this reflected the decision to use existing venues rather than invest in major new projects, and strong leadership and governance structures that ensured projects were well managed and delivered within budget. Or, put in another way, the Games made good use of the investment that had already been made by the City Council as part of its sports and cultural strategies. In this respect, the 2014 Games are one of the least expensive in recent times, and from the city's perspective, the Council contributed £80m to help bring new investment into the city of £382m!

Alternatively, it is possible to view the more than half a billion pounds budget for the Games as money that could have been used differently for the city. This total expenditure, for example, represents half of the total sum invested as part of the 10 year strategy to upgrade the 43,000 social and affordable homes under the Glasgow Housing Association umbrella. Or it is the equivalent of the money spent by the City Council over the last 12 years to improve the city's schools. Both of these are areas of public expenditure that impact on residents throughout the city.

Measuring success

Mindful of this, success for Glasgow had to be more than just a positive experience of 12 days. There had to be a real legacy, one that was shared by the citizens of the city and one that might help to transform the city. The success on the field of play and a positive experience for the hundreds of thousands who watched the events in the city was a vital component. It was a prerequisite for other benefits. But for the City Council the benefits had to be felt across the city and well beyond the arena of sport and culture. The Games gave a chance to advance more quickly than would otherwise have happened projects and investment associated with its strategic priorities. It had to allow local businesses to benefit from the contracts and work associated with the Games and it had to assist those in unemployment or leaving school and education to get opportunities associated with the investment in the Games. For the wider population, the Games had to be a catalyst to encourage people to have more active lifestyles, including through sport and physical activity.

What did the partners want from the Games? For Commonwealth Games Scotland (CGS), the Games were a way to help showcase how investment in elite sport was helping to develop athletes of international standard. And more importantly the Games were a chance to create an argument that, even in times of financial constraint, investment in sport has its rewards for the country as a whole. The success of Team Scotland did not disappoint, with not only the record medal tally meeting the CGS objective, but by also showing how supporting the development of athletes could make the nation feel good about itself. For the Scottish Government, the Games also had to generate legacy, captured within four themes: the opportunity to contribute to the growth of the Scottish economy; to help Scots be more physically active; to strengthen connections at home and internationally through culture and learning; and to demonstrate environmental responsibility and help communities live more sustainably.

The leadership team

To help meet these ambitions, a strong team was created. Indeed one of the widely acknowledged defining characteristics of the Glasgow

2014 Commonwealth Games has been the strong leadership provided by each of the partners and the adoption of an appropriate governance structure to oversee the preparation and delivery of the event.

Within Glasgow key players – such as George Black, Carole Forrest, Lynn Brown, Bridget McConnell and Ian Hooper – have been involved since the start of the bidding process. George Black, Chief Executive of the City Council who retired at the end of 2014, and Bridget McConnell, Chief Executive of Glasgow Life, have been inspirational, ensuring that across both organisations staff have been committed to making the Games work for the city. As a team, they have ensured that the city's approach to the Games connected with the long-term strategies of the city, aligned with its existing capital programmes, its cultural and sports development, and with the economic and communities strategies. They have been supported by the city's politicians, with the leaders of the main party and opposition involved in the governance of the games. The strong commitment from Gordon Matheson – and his predecessor Steven Purcell – as Leader of the Council has helped to unite the city behind the Games whilst the key role of the Depute Leader, Archie Graham as the city's executive member for the Commonwealth Games has been central to planning and developing the Games' legacy.

At the national level, the support from the First Ministers of Scotland – initially Jack McConnell and then Alex Salmond – has been an essential component in presenting a national, united and passionate case to persuade the CGF to back the Glasgow bid, and in the delivery phase to ensure that the benefits reached out across the country. The First Ministers have been supported by a team of ministers with Shona Robison as sports minister in the last few years having a key role in facilitating effective oversight of the plans for the Games. Beyond government, the leadership and stability provided by Louise Martin, Jon Doig and Michael Cavanagh at Commonwealth Games Scotland (CGS) has been vital. Louise and Jon have been central players since the initial 'dream' of Scotland hosting the Games again in 2014 (see Chapter 1), and all three have been passionate at ensuring that athletes were at the centre of the Games and for Team Scotland that home 'advantage' was used to support Scottish sport.

Such continuity of leadership is rare in major sporting event planning, and for most observers has been a key dimension of the success of the Glasgow Games. Public recognition of these central roles was given in the New Year's honours list in 2015, when Bridget McConnell and Gordon Matheson were awarded CBEs and Archie Graham and Jon Doig awarded OBEs.

Glasgow's Commonwealth Games: behind the scenes

THE KEY ORGANISATIONS – AND THE ACRONYMS

- Glasgow City Council (GCC)
- Scottish Government
- Commonwealth Games Scotland (CGS)
- Commonwealth Games Federation (CGF)
- Renamed from Commonwealth Games Council for Scotland (CGCS)
- Commonwealth Games Associations (CGAs)
- Glasgow 2014 Ltd, Organising Committee (OC)
- Glasgow City Marketing Bureau (GCMB)
- Glasgow Life
- Cordia
- Creative Scotland
- Police Scotland
- Transport Scotland

Perhaps one of the most challenging aspects of planning and delivering a major sporting event such as the Commonwealth Games is balancing the needs and aspirations of the host city and the requirements of the international governing body which manages the wider Games movement (the CGF). At each Games, the needs of the CGF are largely managed by an Organising Committee (OC) which the CGF views as independent of the host city and nation, and there to protect the needs of the international athletic movement. The OC thus needs to have strong leadership too. David Grevemberg, the CEO of the OC for most of the 2014 Games, is seen to have achieved just such a (near impossible) balance, widely praised for his leadership by the Scottish and Glasgow partners, by the OC team and the CGF (so much so that he has now moved to be CEO of the CGF). He was supported by Robert Smith, Lord Smith of Kelvin, as chair of the Board of the OC, who drew on his extensive business managerial experience to maintain a strong working relationship with national and local partners. This does not, of course, mean that there have not been disagreements (there are examples of these throughout this book). Contemporary public policy emphasises the importance of 'partnership working' but does so often without acknowledging that tensions and differing priorities are inherent in the process – and that, in fact, resolving these conflicts is what good partnership working is about. The leadership team at the Games proved the value of this.

Making the 'best Games ever'

There are many different ways in which the success of the Games in Glasgow could be evaluated, but perhaps the reasons why the CGF felt able to give the accolade of 'best Games ever' reflected the fact that for everyone involved – as participants, as spectators, from the CGF and the Commonwealth, from Scotland and from within Glasgow – the event delivered on their priorities.

This book's story

This book's focus is from within the city of Glasgow and the City Council family, reflecting the role and experience of the author as research adviser during the Games. While much credit has been given to the 1400 staff employed by the body that organised the Games (OC) and the 12,500 volunteers who supported them, this book explores the contribution of the organisations based in the city to delivering the Games. Most stories of major sporting events focus on the role of the Organising Committee and specialist teams and shed little light on the key contribution of existing public bodies of government. In Glasgow, the Council Family's role has been pivotal, both in terms of preparation of the city to bid for the Games, but also as a major partner in the Games' delivery.

> **Did you know?**
> As well as the City Council, the Council Family includes Glasgow Life (responsible for sport and culture), Community Safety Glasgow, Cordia (responsible for school catering and home care), Glasgow City Marketing Bureau, Clyde Gateway Urban Regeneration Company, City Parking, City Property, ACCCESS (providing ICT and property services), City Building, and Jobs & Business Glasgow.

The focus on the city's contribution comes with a risk of 'writing out' the role and contribution of other partners beyond the city. This is not intentional and, throughout, the role of others partners is woven into the account and hopefully acknowledged. The 2014 story has been one where party politics and political differences between Glasgow City Council and the Scottish Government were not dominant, and indeed differences of opinion were often harnessed to help create a more successful event.

Just as the Games as a sporting event is often defined by the contribution of a few key people who achieve medals or acclaim, this book marks the contribution of certain key people. Some of them have been interviewed for this book, some are acknowledged individually, some have been involved from the start of the story, and others have joined on the way. But, as with the Games as a whole, the event's success relies on many others who take part and contribute. So too here, for there are many others having managerial, operational and leadership roles who are not named but have been important in shaping and delivering the wider success of the Games. And there are thousands of others who had roles during the Games, and in the planning and preparation work. Without all of them, the success of Glasgow's Commonwealth Games would not have been possible.

This book provides an account of why the president of the CGF, Prince Imran, felt able to praise the Glasgow 2014 Games as the 'best ever', and highlights the impact on the city of gathering so many people from across the world into Glasgow in the summer of 2014. It explores how such success was achieved, and considers some of the lessons learnt by those involved. In doing so, it reveals some of the obstacles that have had to be met and overcome in planning the event. And it provides a unique insight into some of the challenges which have had to be met in delivering a successful event.

Drawing on the first-hand experiences of the senior people involved in making the Games, this book offers learning and lessons – for other cities who are considering being a host for a major event; for the partners involved in Scotland and Glasgow; for Glasgow as it looks forward to a new period after the Games.

And it tells a story of how the 2014 Commonwealth Games fits into the longer term transformation of Glasgow, from its past industrial contributions to the world, to one where sport and culture are contributing to the city's image as a modern, vibrant, positive and flourishing place to live and work.

"One of the strengths recognised in the Glasgow story has been the long term commitment and involvement of a few people who have steered everyone to bring about success"

Chapter 1:
Leading the city to the Games

Planning and delivering an event of the size and complexity of the Commonwealth Games is challenging and few cities and nations either have the capacity or the commitment required to take on the task. For Glasgow, hosting the Games in 2014 was both an exciting and stimulating experience for those involved, offering opportunities to learn lessons, gain confidence and help the city continue to be transformed. It has also been a testing and, at times, tense experience, where there has been a need to have a clear vision of purpose and commitment from leaders to ensure that inevitable problems are overcome.

This chapter outlines the contribution of some of these key leaders, their organisations and their involvement in the Games - from the initial development of the idea of a bid from Glasgow and Scotland, through the processes that were developed to plan and deliver the Games, and those who have helped to ensure that the Games has a positive legacy for the city and its citizens. From the initial few key people who helped to set out the vision, the forms of leadership have changed as thousands of people became involved either on a paid or voluntary basis. And this story reveals one of the key strengths recognised in the Glasgow story - the long term commitment and involvement of a few people who have steered everyone to bring about success.

Some of these people will be familiar; others have a less public profile, but all have helped to make the Games. They have rightly been acknowledged for their roles as leaders, but they would be quick to point out (and have done before) that Glasgow's Games were a team effort.

Image 10:
Awaiting the Influx of
Visitors, George Square

Image 11:
Member of the
Govanhill community
participating in the
Cultural Programme

Glasgow's Commonwealth Games: behind the scenes

Getting to the start line

The possibility of Scotland hosting a future Commonwealth Games had its origins in the Manchester 2002 Commonwealth Games. Since Scotland hosted the event in 1970 and 1986 in Edinburgh, the nature of the Games has changed. Not only has the sporting element expanded, but it has grown into one of the top international events attracting television audiences in the billions. It has also become a much larger and more expensive event to host, with host nations and cities investing millions of pounds and having to attract considerable commercial sponsorship

Attending the Manchester Games, Dr Bridget McConnell and Ian Hooper from the City Council's Cultural and Leisure Services had been impressed by the way that Manchester had provided a magical atmosphere which brought sporting success alongside a celebration of the character of the city. For them, Manchester showed how it was possible to bring people into the event – whether through the cultural quarters around the nightlife, clubs and theatres, or as beneficiaries of the regeneration which was being catalysed by the Games. The Manchester experience showed that the Games was more than just a sporting event, but also a landmark in the renewal of a major city.

As the host city and the main partner involved in the Games, Manchester City Council and the organising committee, Manchester 2002 Ltd, set out with the vision of using the 10 days of sporting competition to help use investment in sports facilities and the associated infrastructure to regenerate a large area of East Manchester. Like Glasgow, this area had experienced economic hardship as the manufacturing and industrial base of the area, Manchester and the wider North West region of England, had changed. Using the concept of Sportcity, a concentration of sporting facilities and venues, the games partners sought to breathe new life into the area. Through the development of world class venues and making these available to local communities and grass-root sport, the Manchester approach sought to ensure from the planning stages that there was a physical legacy for the city.

Musing over this in the Scottish team hotel, Bridget McConnell and Ian Hooper – along with government and Scottish Commonwealth Games representatives and former Chief Executive of Sport Scotland Alan Alstead – had a 'what if...' conversation asking whether Glasgow could do the same as Manchester. Reflecting on the investment the city had already made on sporting and cultural facilities (see Chapter 2), the conversation firmed up the initial dreams of Glasgow hosting a future Games with a vision of offering a different form of sporting event that reached out beyond the Games to provide a strong legacy for Glasgow, and to celebrate Glasgow's character and spirit. And they left the meeting with a clear sense that Glasgow could emulate the Manchester experience, building on the City Council's investment in facilities and its passion to connect sport and culture with social and economic regeneration.

The next morning, in a similar vein, another 'what if' moment occurred when Louise Martin, chair of the Commonwealth Games Council for Scotland (CGCS), Jon Doig, also at CGCS, and the First Minister Jack McConnell met at breakfast. For them, the opportunities offered by the Manchester experience focussed on the city's success in galvanising urban and social regeneration around their role as host city and the tangible advantages on the sporting field from home support for Team Scotland. For these three leaders, this provided a potent mix that got them thinking of future possibilities for Scotland.

Returning to Glasgow, Bridget McConnell and Ian Hooper presented their vision of a bid for the Commonwealth Games being part of the city's longer term plan to regenerate communities and enhance its international reputation. This vision - a key element of the legacy from the Games - was crucial in persuading first the senior officials and then elected members of the Council that a bid would provide lasting benefits.

With the support of Glasgow City Council's Chief Executive George Black, and the then Leader of the Council, Stephen Purcell, a team of officials was created to take forward thinking about what a Commonwealth Games bid might look like. Importantly most of these key leaders have continued to be guiding and consistent advocates, playing key roles in the process of bidding and then delivery of the Games. Along with George Black, senior officials in the Council have led the process. Carole Forrest (Assistant Director of Corporate Services) has helped ensure that benefits and legacies from the Games are consistent with the strategic priorities for development of the Council. Lynn Brown (executive director of financial services) has been instrumental in ensuring that capital programmes were delivered within budget, and in coordinating the overall budget management for the city. Under their guidance, the vision of the Games as a vital part of the city's wider plans for regeneration has gained support, and importantly allowed each service area of the Council to see how they could contribute to the successful Games. They also ensured that expenditure was effective in delivering the facilities for the Games but that these would have value for the city before and after the event.

Bridget McConnell and Ian Hooper, now Chief Executive and director of sport and special projects respectively in Glasgow Life, have been instrumental in guiding the planning for the Games to maximise the sporting and cultural benefits for the city. Their internationally recognised expertise and leadership locally has been crucial in balancing the need to meet the requirements of the CGF with the desires of the city.

Political support from the Leader of the Council Gordon Matheson and his depute Archie Graham, as well as from the leaders of the opposition groups in the City Council, has been essential to ensure that over the many years of planning and delivery of the Games there has been a clear and consistent purpose. Archie Graham in particular has been a key contributor in ensuring that across the different committees and organisations set up for the Games the City Council's desire for legacy has been to the fore. In addition to chairing the Council's Glasgow 2014 Group, he has, with support from the dedicated Council 2014 Team, ensured there has been a coordinated approach across the many working groups within the Council to deliver on the legacy goals. In addition, as the Council's executive member for the Commonwealth Games, a member of the Glasgow 2014 (OC) Board, and also on the Board of Glasgow Life, he has been pivotal in managing relationships between the Council and other Games partners.

Preparing for the Games

During the development of the bid from Glasgow on behalf of Scotland to be host for the 2014 Commonwealth Games, an effective partnership structure developed between the City Council, the Scottish Government and Commonwealth Games Scotland. United in the shared goal of developing a high quality and robust bid, the partners developed the local governance structures.

At the national level, corporate governance was led by the First Minister who chaired the 2014 Committee which was established in early 2006. It had responsibility for the strategic direction of the Glasgow 2014 bid and included representatives from the senior officers of the City Council and CGS alongside senior civil servants in support. One key role of this group was to liaise with senior government officials, the Scottish Parliament and other political party leaders to provide the necessary guarantees required as part of the bid. It also assisted in identifying the public funding that would be required to help deliver promises in the bid, and enabled support from other public agencies such as SportScotland and Scottish Enterprise to be drawn into supporting the bid.

With the main focus being on Glasgow, the Glasgow 2014 Working Group chaired by the Chief Executive of the City Council George Black had a key role in drawing together the expertise and knowledge within the Council and the city to help support the bid team, led by Derek Casey. He had been appointed as an external bid director to lead the partners and had a key role in writing the successful bid for the Games (see Chapter 3). Derek Casey had a strong pedigree in supporting sport development in Britain and provided the necessary combination of international knowledge with local expertise. In doing this, the Glasgow team departed from the approach used for most other Commonwealth Games or Olympics where expertise was drawn primarily from outside the host city or nation. The Working Group had the advantage that Glasgow City Council had already accumulated considerable experience in hosting major events. This enabled, for most of the bid development stage, leadership and expertise to be drawn from within the City Council.

On reflection, this bringing together of local staff was a bold, risky but highly successful approach. Importantly it enabled them to work effectively as a team, learning to build on each other's strengths and to use their existing networks in government and beyond to be efficient in meeting the tight deadlines that were required when constructing the bid. In addition, it allowed a growing sense of confidence to emerge in the team about the feasibility of Glasgow being capable of hosting the Games. This grew steadily throughout 2006 as the bid was drafted, rewritten and fine-tuned. But perhaps of greatest significance was the ability to capture local knowledge about venues, operational issues and possible solutions to challenges that external experts would have struggled to know about. The end result was that in putting together the bid, the bid team, the Glasgow 2014 Working Group, and the 2014 Committee developed an effective form of governance that could be used in the later stages to deliver the Games.

Even with this experience, putting together the Commonwealth Games bid was a larger and more complex project than any previously undertaken by the Council and there was a recognition that external expertise around mega-events would be required to take forward the bid once Glasgow was successful.

Bringing international expertise to Glasgow
Moving from candidate city to host city in 2007 having won the right to be the location of the 2014 Games required considerably more expertise than had been available up to that point. The plans outlined in the bid now had to be made operational.

The approach to this process, expected by the Commonwealth Games Federation, is the formation of an Organising Committee or Company (OC), which takes on the primary role of Games delivery. This represents a legally independent entity at 'arms length' from national and local organisations, including government and the national Games Association.

In many respects, this provides a (logical) working structure with the OC offering advantages over the local authority in terms of financial separation and budgetary control (a key dimension for the CGF). This separation also potentially made it easier to get investments from external parties which the City Council may not generate, especially in relation to sponsorship. And it provides a structure within which the skills and expertise required for the Games can be recruited. In addition, as was evident at different points during the last seven years, the creation of an OC separate from the existing governance structures, enables them to have a 'brokering role' between the City Council and Scottish Government. The formation of an OC also acknowledges that most host cities do not have all the necessary specialist expertise in Games delivery to call upon. In many respects, Glasgow was fortunate to have considerable local expertise, but the OC complemented this with other skills and knowledge that helped to make the Games so successful.

On the other hand, the creation of a separate entity risks losing contacts which are already established locally, and this entity can often struggle to find ways to harness the strong local knowledge and culture which the City Council family offers. It creates an additional level of bureaucracy and organisation building for the host city. And it risks losing momentum generated during the bid process.

For 2014, the CGF requirements were that an OC had to be formed as part of the bid process, and an Organising Committee company named Glasgow 2014 Limited was incorporated on 11 June, 2007 as the organisation formally delivering the Games. Each of the OCs and national Games Associations involved in the previous Commonwealth Games had underlined the need for strong leadership to ensure effective working with local organisations, and to drive forward quickly the planning needed for an event of this size and complexity. Glasgow 2014 Ltd as OC was organised as having a board led by a chair which brought together representatives from all the main partners and an executive team led by a CEO. The executive team was responsible for all the operational issues, bringing together expertise not only on event management and sport, but also corporate affairs and business.

Image 12:
View from the Glasgow University tower of the Kelvingrove Lawn Bowls Centre

Image 13:
Commonwealth Games celebrations at Glasgow Green

Glasgow's Commonwealth Games: behind the scenes

THE GLASGOW 2014 LTD BOARD

- Rt Hon Lord Smith of Kelvin *(Chair)*
  Chair of SSE and UK Green Investment Bank
- Louise Martin *(Vice Chair)*
  Commonwealth Games Scotland: Past Chair CGS
- Rhona Simpson
  Athlete Representative: Scotland Coach
- Michael Cavanagh
  Commonwealth Games Scotland: Chairman CGS
- Francesca Osowska
  *Scottish Government: Director of Housing,
  Regeneration & Commonwealth Games*
- John Mason
  Scottish Government: Director of Business
- Cllr Archie Graham
  Glasgow City Council: Depute Leader and Executive Member for Culture & Sport
- Dr Bridget McConnell
  Glasgow City Council: CEO Glasgow Life
- Eileen Gallagher
  Independent Director: CEO Shed Productions
- Sir Bill Gammell
  Independent Director: Cairn Energy
- Colin Hood
  Independent Director: Scottish & Southern Energy
- Alan Mitchelson
  Independent Director: Weir Group

Planning for the Glasgow 2014 OC started immediately after the announcement that Glasgow would be host city. The appointment of a chair to the OC Board was considered by the Strategic Group, led by the First Minister, in late 2007. Shortlisted candidates had met with the First Minister, Louise Martin, and Steven Purcell (then leader of Glasgow City Council) on 31 January 2008 and they identified Robert Smith, Lord Smith of Kelvin, as the preferred candidate. With his appointment in place, he then was involved in the selection of the CEO of Glasgow 2014 which had been advertised in January 2008.

To help achieve this, in many major sporting events it had been common for the head of the bid team or company to be offered the position of CEO at the OC, ensuring continuity of purpose and vision, and retaining the network of relationships which have been a necessary and vital part of constructing a bid. Ron Walker (Melbourne,

2006) and Mark Peters (Gold Coast, 2018) in relation to the Commonwealth Games, and John Furlong (Vancouver Winter Olympics, 2010), and Sebastian Coe (London Summer Olympics, 2012) each led the bid teams and then the OC. However, this was not going to be possible in Glasgow as Derek Casey, the bid director, had signalled that he was not seeking this position.

Following open recruitment, John Scott was appointed as CEO in April 2008. Although not involved in the Glasgow bid, he had a strong pedigree having previously been on the board of the Manchester 2002 Games and advisor on the London 2012 bid, as well as involved with previous unsuccessful bids in other cities around the world.

Under John Scott and Robert Smith's guidance, the OC sought to get itself established quickly, allowing the bid plans to be turned into a 7 year plan for delivery of the Games. Although John Scott left the OC in 2009, the planning process was well underway and his successor David Grevemberg was already part of the OC team. And David Grevemberg brought important continuity having initially been appointed as director of operations for Glasgow 2014 but then serving as chief operations officer.

Did you know?
As a former wrestler, David Grevemberg, the CEO of Glasgow 2014 OC, had been director of sport for the International Paralympic Committee developing the programme of sports for the Paralympic Games. Since the end of the Glasgow Games, David has been appointed as Chief Executive officer of the Commonwealth Games Federation.

Throughout the process of delivering the Games there has been a shared ambition for the Glasgow Games to be successful as an event. As illustrated in some of the key facts and figures in the introduction to this book, on many measures the Games fulfilled these ambitions. However, in the period between the bid in 2007 and the Games in 2014, the path to such success has not always been easy, with occasional tensions created by the different ambitions of the partners involved. Resolving these and creating the effective collaboration that has been a key characteristic of the partnership working has required strong leadership and willingness to compromise so that together the ambitions for the Games were met.

THE MAIN AMBITIONS OF GAMES PARTNERS

- Glasgow City Council – creating a legacy for the city and the Games helping to drive forward change and development across Glasgow

- Scottish Government – supporting GCC's ambitions and ensuring that benefits from the Games reached across the country

- Commonwealth Games Scotland – ensure strong sporting performances from Team Scotland, and support development of the values and ethos of the Commonwealth Games

- Glasgow 2014 Ltd (OC) – deliver an athlete-centred Games and a high quality experience for all those involved

One early example of this arose around the issue of a Games legacy. The desire to ensure that Games provide longer term and measurable benefits was a strong driving force behind the City Council and Scottish Government's ambitions and, from the start of the bid process, it had been an essential outcome from the Games. Expressed both as legacy and in the relationship of the Games with the routine business of government, there was an expectation that throughout the planning for the Games, legacy would be prominent. This notion of legacy and mainstreaming (that is, making it central to all aspects of the planning and preparation of the event) was something that was different to undertakings by previous host cities - and very different to the experience of OC staff.

> **Did you know?**
> The Commonwealth Games are also known as the 'Friendly Games' and underlying the Games are three core values - humanity, equality and destiny - helping to inspire and unite people through sport and culture.

In the early days, the OC did not share this focus, suggesting that legacy was not the key function of the OC and solely the responsibility of the City Council and the Scottish Government. This was a view which led to several clashes in the early days with other partners. Gradually, and assisted by the appointment of David Grevemberg as replacement CEO in 2010, the OC took an active role in supporting the creation of legacies, creating what he termed 'legacy consciousness' to inform the roles and functions of the OC.

In other respects, however, the OC's focus on the needs of athletes and on Games delivery assisted other partners. With a strong lead to ensure that Games were delivered within budget, there was pressure on the OC to be prudent. However, in early 2014 when plans were well advanced, there was a sense within the City Council that opportunities to make the best Games ever were being lost because of financial pressures. The Council's Chief Executive George Black intervened and, with the support of additional expenditure, impressed on the OC the need to move from a competent Games to making it the best possible.

One of the hardest challenges for an OC is gaining enough of an understanding and appreciation of the local context and, in particular, the relevant expertise that had been accumulated there quickly. With the OC recruiting staff on the basis of international event delivery and management experience, less attention is given to familiarity with local contexts. Glasgow 2014 OC too recruited extensively from beyond the city and very few of the people involved in the bid process were brought into the OC. As a result, a repeated refrain in the early days of planning was 'this was not how it was done in...' followed by Manchester, Vancouver, Sydney or another host city where the OC staff had been involved with a major event.

This was a lost opportunity. The OC could have gained from the experience and expertise in event management that was already to be found in the City Council and Glasgow Life, and drawn on the practical knowledge such as fire safety, lighting, public access and queue management at venues that the Glasgow teams had learnt from hosting previous events. But it was also a missed opportunity for the City Council to ensure local staff were included in key roles in the OC. The momentum which had been built during the bidding process (see Chapter 3) was lost as the Council did not capitalise on encouraging more local staff to be part of the OC.

The consequence of this was that much time and energy was used by all partners in reinforcing the central goals of the Glasgow and Scottish Government priorities, revisiting many decisions as the increasingly large and complex OC tried to get staff to appreciate the importance of local desires and the core value of legacies. Whilst this was evident in some aspects of the Games delivery, through time the partners have developed a mutual respect for each other, working towards a shared desire to deliver a great Games and to provide local benefits.

Image 15:
Glasgow's Gallery
of Modern Art

Image 16:
Festival 2014 events
on Glasgow Green

Glasgow's Commonwealth Games: behind the scenes

Stability and change

Achieving stability in leadership over such a long time period – 7 years from selection as host city to the Games – is challenging, with change in political leadership at national and local level almost inevitable, and with other partners likely to experience change at their senior levels too.

One of the features of the Glasgow experience has been the high level of stability in its leadership. Within the Council, senior officials including George Black, Carole Forrest and Lynn Brown were involved throughout, and elected member Councillor Archie Graham has provided a strong and consistent link as executive member for the Commonwealth Games and by serving on the OC Board. In Glasgow Life, Dr Bridget McConnell, Ian Hooper (Director of Sport and Capital Projects) and Jill Miller (Director of Cultural Services) were also involved in the initial bid team and had central roles across the cultural and sport programmes in the Games. And Louise Martin has been a stable force in the Commonwealth Games Council for Scotland throughout the period of the Games. Similarly in the Scottish Government team, there has been continuity with Diane McLafferty leading the Scottish Government's Games division for much of the period. This continuity of leadership – and indeed of many of the staff within key teams – has been acknowledged by many of those involved as invaluable, allowing strong and harmonious working relationships to be fostered and ensuring a focus on the long-term perspective of benefits from being host to the Games. In turn, this has helped to create a more collaborative working environment, reducing moments of disagreement or potential conflict, and allowing them to be resolved through dialogue.

Previous experiences for other host cities suggest that OCs are frequently subject to change in key personnel, reflecting in part the time-limited nature of their existence. The Manchester 2002 OC was noted for its strong record of staff retention at all levels, but this was the exception. Other OCs have experienced staff losses at senior levels in the later stages of preparation for mega-sport events – and there was some of this in Glasgow.

After the replacement of John Scott by David Grevemberg as Chief Executive of the OC in 2009, there has been a strong degree of continuity in its top leadership. Both Robert Smith and David Grevemberg have been seen universally as providing effective and consistent leadership, steering the OC and working well with other partners. This has not been easy, given the rapid growth in personnel in the OC up to Games time and the increasing number of other agencies which have to be involved in each of the dimensions of the Games – including working with other local authorities across Scotland for the Queen's Baton Relay (QBR), with Creative Scotland in relation to the cultural programme, Scottish Enterprise for economic and employment goals, and especially Transport Scotland in travel planning.

There have been some changes at other levels in the OC. Where there was time for relationships and the exchange of knowledge to occur at a more operational level, the collaborative model of working with staff in the Council was effective, providing opportunities to share knowledge and to develop solutions to the myriad small issues that are part of event preparation. However, like many OCs as the Games approached and contracts came towards the end, there was some departure of operational staff, including some key people leading functional areas. The accompanying loss of knowledge and personal contacts that had been developed over the preceding months and years with the Council family staff were inevitably lost and pressure to meet deadlines did not always enable new appointees to rebuild such relationships and the shared ethos of generating a legacy for Glasgow and not 'just another Games' at times dissolved.

In Glasgow, the City Council too had undergone change in the same time period, with significant organisational restructuring in the period up to the Games. The formation of Glasgow Life was one – particularly significant – change. In 2006 the Cultural and Leisure Services division of the Council was transferred to an independent charitable organisation to manage and run the sport and cultural facilities in the city, with ownership of the buildings and collections being retained by the Council. As Glasgow Life, the organisation was designed to encourage innovation and creativity, and to bring together sport and culture more coherently for the benefit of local communities. For the Games, Glasgow Life's formation provided a clearer and coherent structure to help develop sporting venues and to make connections between the sporting programmes and the cultural celebrations which were sought by the CGF.

Financial leadership
One of the largest challenges of major sporting events in recent times has been the ability to deliver the event within budget. It is one of the less noteworthy positive aspects of the process used by the CGF that they require potential host cities to specify a budget in their bid which then becomes the benchmark against which the total cost is set; even though not all costs can be rigorously estimated more than seven

years in advance of the event.

There is always an understandable, if at times obsessive, interest in the total costs of hosting an event of this size. With the use of public funds, care for the public interest and accountability is vital and a strong part of the democratic values which the Commonwealth espouses.

And in Glasgow's case there was also understandably even greater interest. In light of the high and greater than planned cost of the London 2012 Olympic and Paralympic Games, there was sensitivity about how such events could be managed within budget. This was heightened not only by competing demands for funding with Glasgow, but by the lack of transparency about costs associated with the Delhi Games in 2010. The alleged separation of costs of flyovers, roads, expansion of the metro and new power plants from the Delhi 'Games budget' reported to the CGF did little to clarify what was the total cost to the local and national taxpayers.

The draft budget in the bid of £275m was quickly revised at the time of the announcement of the selection of Glasgow as host city in 2007, as the experience of planning other Games – both in Delhi and London – helped to clarify the need, for example, for greater security. This was finalised as £575m with a contingency fund of £45.8m and a special reserve being held by the Scottish Government of £23.8m released only with approval from the First Minister. The need for tight cost control measures to deliver the Games within this budget is obvious when the Glasgow 2014 budget is compared with, for example, the £2.5bn cost of the Delhi Games as reported by the auditor general in India.

The shared desire of the leaders from the Games partners to work within this budget inevitably created the need to rein in some aspirations. But it also provided incentives for imaginative ways to manage costs and to increase revenue. The OC for example decided to contract the City Council to deliver the Games venues, meaning that they were able to claim back VAT and reduce the overall cost. This decision also had the advantage of enabling maximum use of the existing procurement skills within the Council and project management expertise within Glasgow Life (a lesson from Manchester 2002) and helping ensure that long-term local use was balanced with temporary use during the Games (a lesson learnt from Delhi 2010).

And in terms of revenue, the OC surpassed the target set in the budget to raise over £110m from commercial revenue – including ticket sales, media rights, and merchandise, despite the impact of the global economic downturn in the lead up to the event. The income raised was more than four times that achieved in Delhi in 2010.

Within the City Council, Lynn Brown and her team in finance recognised that one of the reasons why many previous major events overspent was that capital programmes developing the necessary infrastructure were often delivered too late. With the date of the Games immovable, Games delivery teams faced a choice of either reducing quality or increasing expenditure in order to meet deadlines. Determined not to be faced with such choices, the capital programme in Glasgow started quickly after the decision to bid and all the major elements were in place nearly one year ahead of the Games. Planning projects over a period of 7 or more years, however, generates its own challenges.

One such challenge arose in relation to the development of the Athletes' Village. The plan was that the 'village' would after the Games be used to create new private and socially rented housing for the local community in the Dalmarnock area, and bringing the area back into use (see Chapter 4 for more on the village and community). The City Council managed the initial land reclamation, but a private sector partnership, City Legacy, successfully tendered for the development.

However with the global financial crises from 2008 and the subsequent tightening of loan conditions from major banks to residential development projects, City Legacy found it more difficult than anticipated to get access to cash loans. In a highly imaginative solution, the City Council offered to provide loans from the Strathclyde Pension Fund which it managed, drawing on capital available in the Pension Fund to support local projects which offer an attractive investment opportunity but which are struggling to gain more traditional forms of financial backing. With the approval of the Pension Fund trustees, the funding made available not only secured working capital for City Legacy but also provided a high rate of return on investment for the Pension Fund – and it enabled the Athletes' Village to be completed on time and to be a major legacy for the East End of the city.

The cost of the Games
The Games cost £424.5m. This was £150.5m less than the budget of £575m that had been approved in November 2013.

BUDGET AREA	ALLOCATED BUDGET (£M)	ACTUAL SPEND (£M)
Athletes village and venues	153	148
Games services (e.g. transport, logistics)	58	68
Staff and volunteers	72	70
Broadcasting	31	31
Corporate services	32	35
Technology	38	39
Ceremonies	27	29
Communications and marketing	24	25
Sport	8	8
Safety and security	90	88
Other	2	2
TOTAL	**535**	**543**

Note: these figures do not include expenditure on other venues planned before the Games, including the SSE Hydro, Emirates Arena and Royal Commonwealth Pool refurbishment.

As the final sums for the Games indicate, the financial leadership shown by the partners to operate within their budget helped to address some of the recent scepticism that major sporting events are accompanied by escalating costs. The successful financial outcome was greatly assisted by the contribution from the Council's long term investment in sporting infrastructure, and by the strong public support for the Games through ticket sales which surpassed expectations and resulted in 98% of all available tickets being sold.

Managing the Games delivery

As planning for the Games develops, many more people have to be involved and leadership becomes more devolved. Suitable mechanisms have to be found to share knowledge and data, to provide collaboration on projects, and monitor progress. A complex array of structures has to be put in place to provide such governance and clear lines of communication between them are vital.

In the City Council, the City Operations Board provided a central coordination point; chaired by the Chief Executive and involving all the senior officers, it met regularly to review progress and provide support as required.

But across the partners, many more staff were involved and two of the main challenges were ensuring that 'business as usual' within the Council and its partners continued alongside the Games, and that legacy would be achieved. Illustrating this, the list below reflects some of the Games related projects which the Glasgow Life operations team had to coordinate or support alongside the day-to-day operations of the sporting and cultural activities of the city.

GAMES VENUES	Project managing the building of the 5 Games venues within the city Development planning of venues and options with OC
VENUE USE AGREEMENT	Completing legal contracts for use of the venues by the OC
TRAINING VENUES	Coordinating availability of these venues
CEREMONIES, CULTURE AND QUEEN'S BATON RELAY	Project managing the delivery of these elements in partnership with Creative Scotland, the OC and with the CGS Board
'GLASGOW CELEBRATES'	Development of city projects with OC and GCC
AUDIENCE DEVELOPMENT	Supporting OC in development of ticketing strategy and linking this to opportunities for people to try new sport and cultural activities
HR AND SECONDMENTS	Development of policy for GL staff to be transferred to the OC for periods between months and years
GAMES VOLUNTEERING	Liaison with City Council Operations Board and OC
HOST CITY VOLUNTEERS	Development of citizenship and volunteering project
COMPETITION MANAGEMENT	Continue delivering other events in the city alongside the Games
TEST EVENTS PROGRAMME	Liaison with OC on events which GL mounted
CITY MARKETING	Liaison with GCMB and GCC on city brand
COMMUNITIES	Liaison with OC and GCC on effective involvement of local communities in the city

LEGACY EQUIPMENT	Collaboration with OC on provision of sports equipment for use in city
RESEARCH AND EVALUATION	Commissioning of research on legacy and evaluation of events
MEDIA MANAGEMENT	Collaboration with OC on Games communications
ROAD EVENTS	Joint development of marathon and road race courses with OC and GCC
TRAINING CAMPS	Liaison with SportScotland on provision of facilities
LOOK AND FEEL	Liaison with GCC, GCMB and OC on dressing the city for Games
POST-GAMES EXHIBITION	Organisation of display at People's Palace
COMMONWEALTH SPORTS DEVELOPMENT CONFERENCE	Liaison with OC and CSG on 2010 and 2013 conferences on 'youth sport'
COUNTDOWN CLOCK	Liaison with OC

For senior staff in the City Council, Glasgow Life and GCMB, along with their operational duties they took on responsibility for overseeing the legacies associated with the Council's six main themes (these are discussed in more detail in Chapter 5), ensuring that benefits in each area could be embedded into the regular operations and services.

LEGACY THEME	LEGACY CHAMPION	POSITION
Prosperous	Richard Brown	Executive Director – Development and Regeneration Services
Active	Ian Hooper	Director of Sports and Special Projects – Glasgow Life
International	Scott Taylor	Chief Executive of Glasgow City Marketing Bureau
Greener	Brian Devlin	Executive Director – Land and Environmental Services
Accessible	Brian Devlin	Executive Director – Land and Environmental Services
Inclusive	Maureen McKenna	Executive Director – Education Services

Building success

Planning for a major sporting event in the midst of an economic downturn when public and private sector funding is tight, and when people across the city are struggling through the housing and financial crisis, was always going to be a challenge. This was unexpected at the time of the bid and when crowned 'host city' in 2007. The global financial crisis has added to the importance of a strong steer from the leaders of the Council, Scottish Government and the OC in particular. Not only did the difficult economic circumstances strengthen the determination to deliver the Games on (or below) budget, but they also highlighted the need for a clear and consistent focus on how investment in the Games can have benefits in the long term and help to meet many of the current and longer term needs of Glaswegians.

The leadership provided across all the partners in Glasgow has been significant, and their commitment has been a vital component in making the Games a success. Their personalities too have helped to ensure that the governance and delivery structures which accompany an event of this size worked effectively. With their desire to work in partnership, to be creative in finding solutions and, where necessary, to be persistent but compromising in resolving tensions, they provided the visible commitment that helped to galvanise staff across all the organisations involved with the Games.

Image 18:
Glasgow Arc Bridge,
Morning

Image 19:
Host City Volunteers
help direct visitors in
George Square

Glasgow's Commonwealth Games: behind the scenes

"The Games for Glasgow were an investment for the future, contributing to a much longer-term strategy of change in the city built around sport and culture"

Chapter 2
Glasgow's sporting pedigree

The story of Glasgow's Commonwealth Games has its origins long before the decision to bid to be host city. That step is considered in the next chapter, but the possibility of bidding was only realistic because the City Council had, over several decades, invested in modernising and expanding its sporting and cultural infrastructure. Some of the unique and key aspects of the Glasgow event reflect this history. The fact that it could show that the majority of venues were built and capable of delivering the Games, that the cost of the event would be only a fraction of that required by Delhi to host its Games in 2010, and that the sporting events would be accompanied by a year-long celebration of culture was only possible because of past investment. And in turn, the Games for Glasgow was an investment for the future, contributing to a much longer-term strategy of change in the city built around sport and culture.

This investment in infrastructure also brought the advantage that Glasgow has a strong and proven record of hosting major events. None so large as the Commonwealth Games, but the city did represent national and international competition in many of the sports of the 2014 Games. And often ignored in accounts leading up to the Games, Glasgow's sporting pedigree meant that it had a highly experienced and competent workforce who had the knowledge and skills to help deliver the best Games ever.

From City of Culture to Sports City
In the 1980s, in an attempt to reposition Glasgow economically and to change perceptions of the city, the Council invested in the development of new cultural facilities. This formed part of a long-term strategy of using culture to assist in the regeneration of communities and the city as a whole. In what was one of the first post-industrial cities to

develop a cultural-led regeneration programme, Glasgow's approach became a benchmark followed by others such as Liverpool and Manchester.

A series of initiatives enabled the city to hold single international events as well as more permanent cultural activities. The opening of the Burrell Collection in 1983 in Pollok Park marked the start of this major investment, but it was the opening of the Scottish Exhibition and Conference Centre (SECC) on the site of the former Queen's Docks on the side of the River Clyde in 1985, and the Glasgow Garden Festival in 1988 on the opposite river bank, that signalled more visibly the link between cultural activity and economic and urban regeneration. Since opening, the SECC has become a central venue for the city's delivery of its cultural strategy. The 'precinct' has expanded greatly over the years, with the latest development – the SSE Hydro indoor arena – adding a further 12,500 seats at its opening in 2013. Largely owned by the City Council, the 'precinct' with its large mix of auditoria, seated spaces, arenas, large parking capacity and flexible space makes it an ideal location for major events.

Based on this investment, the City Council bid to be European City of Culture becoming the first city in the UK (and 6th city in Europe) to hold the title in 1990. With millions of people attracted to the city during the year and with significant international attention, the 1990 City of Culture event underlined the potential to use art and culture – and, more widely, major events – as an instrument to help rebuild economically and socially.

Did you know?
The SECC was the main venue of the European Special Summer Olympic Games in 1990. During the Commonwealth Games, the SECC hosted boxing, gymnastics, judo, netball, wrestling and weightlifting and was the location of the international broadcasting centre and the main press centre.

Created with the aim of forging closer cultural ties between European nations, and formally designated as such by the Council of Ministers of the European Union, the European City of Culture event was meant to last for one month each year. Whereas the previous holders of the title had viewed the title as a celebration of past achievements in the cultural sector and arena, Glasgow's 1990 bid was designed as part of a strategic investment programme to ensure the growth of a cultural sector in the city and to transform the city's reputation in the UK and abroad.

Following on from the 1988 Garden Festival, the Year of Culture was also aimed at restoring self-confidence and pride in the city. And the city also decided to celebrate its title by extending the events to cover the whole year.

Did you know?
To support the 1990 City of Culture events, the Council invested in additional cultural infrastructure, opening the Glasgow Royal Concert Hall, renovating the nearby McLellan Galleries, and transforming the derelict Tramway into a performing and visual arts centre. Within one year the economic return to Glasgow was estimated to have been at least £10m and supported the extra employment of at least 5,350 people.

The success of the 1990 event in using culture as a catalyst for urban regeneration was an important key to helping senior officials in Glasgow to appreciate the contribution which could come from being a host city for major events, combined with renewed and new visitor attractions. Following through its year as city of culture, investment has continued with, for example, the Charles Rennie Mackintosh exhibition in 1996 and the Year of Architecture and Design in 1999.

The refurbishment of older, mainly Victorian, cultural attractions in the city - Kelvingrove Museum and Gallery, the Mitchell Library, city theatres and the city halls - helped to reinvigorate its cultural appeal. New attractions included the Gallery of Modern Art (1996), and much more recently the Riverside Museum (2011). The legacy was also a major rise in UK and international tourists visiting Glasgow, growing from 0.8m (UK) and 0.4m (international) in 1991 to 1.4m and 0.5m respectively in 1999, the city's Year of Architecture and Design. And since then tourist numbers have continued to increase, reaching 2.4 million by 2010.

Learning from this cultural turn

Two key lessons from 1990 were important in shaping the City Council's desire to host the 2014 Commonwealth Games. First, there was criticism within the city from community groups, from academics and others that in seeking to redefine the external image of Glasgow, the City of Culture events failed to engage with local communities. Although events were held across the city – reaching 80% of local communities – the focus was primarily seen to be on the city centre (venues) and high art and culture rather than local cultural expression. Only 1% of the budget was used to support local arts events. Even though there was a sustained increase in cultural attendance across all social groups following 1990, the Year of Culture had a greater longer term impact on external perceptions and images of the city than it did on its own citizens.

Second, the 1990 year underlined the need for a continuing focus over the longer term on art and culture to maintain any economic advantage from single events. Other cities in the UK and Europe also invested in cultural programmes and facilities, increasing competition with Glasgow. And growth in the cultural sector in Glasgow slowed as the City Council's financial situation worsened in the late 1990s. Investment in regular events such as Celtic Connections, International Jazz Festival, Merchant City Festival and Glasgow International Festival of Visual Art has been important to retain momentum and external awareness.

The experience of the cultural renaissance in the city however did show that major events and the investment needed to host them can provide both immediate economic and social benefits and longer term legacies. For sustainable regeneration there had to be a long term strategy and commitment to providing the required investment in both local and international culture, in infrastructure renewal, and in regular, locally generated festivals as well as major international events.

Image 21:
Residents participate in Cultural Programme activities in Govanhill Library

Image 22:
Cultural Programme event outside Cardonald Library

Glasgow's Commonwealth Games, behind the scenes

Image 23:
Mental Concentration for the Para-lifting, SECC

Image 24:
10,000m Final – One of the Athletics Highlights, Hampden Park

Glasgow's Commonwealth Games: behind the scenes

Image 27:
Festivities on
Glasgow Green

Image 28:
Glasgow's City Centre
transformed by the buzz
created by the Games
and the sunshine

Adding a sporting dimension

The success of the cultural strategy in assisting economic and social regeneration encouraged senior officials at Glasgow City Council to extend an 'events and infrastructure strategy' to include sport - one based on a similar approach of investment across the city to provide modern, international-standard facilities able to attract major sporting events whilst also updating and upgrading facilities for Glaswegians. Like a few other cities across the world, including Melbourne, Glasgow City Council took the radical step of bringing together its sports and leisure services, cultural and arts services and museums into a single unit, Cultural & Leisure Services - which in 2004 became Glasgow Life.

This bold move, driven in part by financial necessity, offered the Council an opportunity to add a sporting dimension to the city's cultural event calendar, and to seek to use both sport and culture to help address some of the deep-seated problems in the city - poor health, low levels of physical activity, social inequalities and high levels of unemployment.

From 1998 to 2002, ambitious proposals for investment in sport facilities to help both the development of sport locally and wider community regeneration were discussed with sporting agencies across Scotland. Support for the city's strategy was harnessed as these agencies too shared the vision for the city, with major grants from the Heritage, Arts and Sports Lottery Funds augmenting the significant investment by the Council of its own funds. Whilst not all the proposals were universally welcomed - the closure of local Victorian swimming baths in particular were controversial - the Council's investment created more modern facilities, able to host national and international events.

Did you know?
As well as facilities for the Commonwealth Games, Glasgow City Council had investment in major sports facilities at Crownpoint Sports Complex (1984), Tollcross Leisure Centre (1997), Nethercraigs Sports Complex (2005), Toryglen Regional Football Centre (2009), and Scotstoun Stadium (2010).

Although most of this initiative had been funded by the City Council, an opportunity to take forward regeneration through sport was extended by the possibility of gaining support for new infrastructure under the Scottish Government's national sports facility review in 2002. In 1998, the creation of a devolved government in Scotland meant that responsibility for sports and the arts was passed to the newly formed Scottish Parliament. A new national body – Sport-Scotland – was formed to invest in sport, drawing on funding from the Scottish Government and distributing National Lottery funding for sport in Scotland with sport linked explicitly to the National Cultural Strategy and Physical Activity Strategy. With the publishing of a second Sport 21 strategy in 2002, sport was both a key policy area and one that was intertwined with the future of the nation.

Did you know?
Glasgow has the largest civic sports infrastructure in the UK, including 12 swimming pools and 22 gyms, and provides more than 1000 fitness classes each week.

In relation to the 2014 Commonwealth Games, however, it was the decision by the Scottish Executive to instruct SportScotland to conduct a review in 2002 of national facilities that was most significant. This review, primarily driven to ensure value for money and to consider the need for realignment of funding across the sport sector by government, was conducted to identify objectives for both wider participation in sport and further selective support for elite performance of some sports. From the perspective of the bid for the 2014 Games, this review was both timely and essential. It identified how an alignment of new investment in facilities of national and international standard was essential to enable the combined benefits of supporting elite athletes and enabling them to compete on home territory at this level. As well as identifying the need for regional and municipal facilities, the review indicated priorities in relation to national facilities.

National Sports Facility Strategy 1997-2004

KEY FACILITIES IDENTIFIED AS NEEDED	OUTCOMES	LOCATION
Regional indoor training facility	National sports training centre Regional football centre Scotstoun Leisure Centre	Largs, Inverclyde Toryglen, Glasgow Glasgow

National indoor sports arena	Emirates Arena	Glasgow
Indoor velodrome	Sir Chris Hoy Velodrome	Glasgow
National training centre for curling	National Curling Centre	Stirling
50m completion swimming pool	Tollcross International Swimming Centre	Glasgow
National sports halls	National Performance Centre for Sport	Riccarton, Edinburgh

For Glasgow City Council, having developed its own sport event strategy, the national review offered opportunities to secure further investment in major sporting facilities. At that time Glasgow was using the Kelvin Hall International Sports Arena to host major indoor sporting events, Tollcross Leisure Centre for international standard swimming facilities and Scotstoun Stadium for outdoor track and field events as the main homes for outdoor athletics competition. All three were becoming outdated and needing refurbishment. Locally too, sports facilities were suffering from years of under-investment. Local swimming baths across the city for example dated mainly from the Victorian period and had declining numbers of users, whilst the facilities for outdoor sports including football and athletics were primarily associated with school playing fields. And facilities for other sports such as tennis, netball, basketball and squash were almost entirely provided by the private and commercial sectors, and located in the more affluent areas of the city.

As well as these larger facilities, the City Council and Glasgow Life had been investing in upgrading and expanding community based facilities. New fitness suites and facilities for gym members of the 'Glasgow Club' – the membership scheme for residents run by Glasgow Life – had been opened, some as part of school complexes and investment made in the lead up to the Games of two Super Gyms. Local fitness classes and guidance, modern equipment and trained staff form the basis of a citywide effort to increase fitness and healthy lifestyles.

This investment and improvement in facilities means that Glasgow has the largest civic sports complex in the UK. Its achievements have been rewarded with significantly increased local participation and by external recognition, including European City of Sport 2003 and, in 2010, it was ranked 8th in the world for major sports events in the SportBusiness Ultimate Sports City Awards and has remained in the top ten since then.

Main community sports facilities, Glasgow

MAJOR CENTRES	LARGE COMMUNITY CENTRE	GLASGOW CLUB LOCAL FACILITIES	GLASGOW CLUB LOCAL FACILITIES LINKED TO SCHOOLS
Toryglen Football Centre	Bellahouston Super Gym	Donald Dewar Leisure Club	Haghill
Scotstoun Stadium	Gorbals Super Gym	Maryhill	Holyrood
Scotstoun Leisure Centre	Crownpoint Sports Complex	Milton Community Campus	John Paul
Tollcross International Swimming Centre	Castlemilk Pool and Leisure Centre	Nethercraigs	Drumoyne
National Hockey Centre	Easterhouse Pool and Glasgow Cub	North Woodside	Whitehill
Emirates Indoor Arena	Palace of Art	Pollok	
Sir Chris Hoy Velodrome	Petershill	Yoker	
Kelvingrove Park Bowling Centre	Springburn Pool and Gym		

As a result of this combination of investments, by the time of the bid for the Commonwealth Games, Glasgow had 70% of the required sports facilities in place, already serving local people and hosting international events. Significantly too, in making the city a key location for supporting national sport, most of the new facilities were meeting needs identified in the national strategy to support key sports in Scotland.

Did you know?
In advance of the start of the Games, the Emirates Arena complex had seen average monthly use grow from 30,000 when it opened in 2012 to 41,000 in early 2014.

The Emirates Arena, one of the more recent additions to the sporting facilities landscape was opened nearly 2 years before the Games and by the summer of 2014 had already been the venue for major sporting competitions across a wide variety of major sports. Its flexibility as an indoor arena had already enabled national and international competitions in badminton, judo, netball, basketball, wrestling, boxing and athletics to be hosted there. The Sir Chris Hoy Velodrome had hosted the UCI Track Cycling World Cup, along with national competitions. But the arena is also a community resource, providing fitness suites and classes, meeting spaces, a café and offices for the local Glasgow Life team and is headquarters for the governing body Netball Scotland. Since opening, more than 40,000 visits were being made each month, and almost half of these were by members of the Glasgow Club.

Similar experiences existed in the other new venues. The National Hockey Centre at Glasgow Green has become the home of Scottish Hockey, providing training and games facilities for local clubs and schools. Cathkin Braes Mountain Bike Trails have accommodated not only the increasing public interest in mountain biking but also the Mountain Trail Bike Cross Country National Championships in June 2013. The SSE Hydro, built to extend the Scottish Exhibition and Conference Centre complex and which combined sport and cultural use, had already attracted large audiences with its varied entertainment programme.

SOME MAJOR GAMES MILESTONES

June 2011	M74 completion opened
September 2011	Commonwealth House opened as Glasgow 2014 HQ
October 2012	Emirates Arena opened
May 2013	Tollcross International Swimming Centre opened
June 2013	Cathkin Braes Mountain Bike Trail opened
July 2013	Glasgow Green Hockey Centre opened
September 2013	SSE Hydro opened

Using the Venues for the Games

Having existing venues in place or planned for most of the sports in the Commonwealth Games was a strong card to play when bidding (see next chapter) – reducing risks of new stadia not being completed and reducing the overall cost of the Games. But this also created different challenges at Games time, including the need to move existing users to other venues disruption that would not be present if the venues had been built exclusively for international events. On the positive side, the venues have been well tested and used and staff have local knowledge and skills. Secondly, existing venues have to be adapted to meet the Games' needs – what is termed overlay – but that was compensated for by the much lower cost than if the facility had to be built anew. And thirdly, the usual approach of handing over responsibility to the organisers of the Games for them to manage them as Game venues was difficult when the City Council, Glasgow Life and other stadia managers had to keep the venues open to communities.

In Glasgow a different and often innovative approach has had to be taken, both in the adjustments made to stadia for the Games, and the way in which the process in managed (see Chapter 3). One example – the transformation of Hampden from home of football into a world class athletics facility – highlights the challenge that using existing venues brings.

Most host cities recognise the central importance symbolically and in sporting terms of the track and field events. These traditionally attract some of the greatest media attention and attendances at the Games. As a result the provision of a stadium with sufficient capacity and facilities is a vital element of a successful bid. For most cites the response has been one of either a new build (e.g. the Manchester Stadium in 2002) or using an already constructed stadium which has housed track and field events in the past – such as the Jawaharlal Nehru stadium in Delhi or the MCG in Melbourne.

The absence of such a stadium in Glasgow meant that an alternative approach had to be taken. The possibility of using either of the two main football stadia – for Rangers and Celtic Football Clubs – was not an option, whilst Hampden had not previously been used for athletics because the infield area is too small. The option of a new stadium was ruled out, both in terms of the initial cost, and in the absence of a sustainable long term use for a dedicated athletics stadium.

The innovative solution developed during the bid process was to construct a platform floor and track 1.9m above the existing pitch, removing some of the seating to allow space for facilities that meet the International Amateur Athletics Federation (IAAF) standard.

With the technology and structures having never been used on this scale, there was a degree of risk in the venture. But rigorous testing and careful construction resulted in one of the top class venues for athletics, acclaimed by the spectators (who got really close to the athletes) and the athletes (for the atmosphere and facilities). The innovative approach has attracted considerable attention from the IAAF as this now opens up the possibility of similar conversions – temporary or permanent – to occur in other cities and for other athletic events.

For Glasgow, although only a temporary facility, the City Council has ensured that this solution has provided an athletic legacy. The track and the warm up facility in the neighbouring Lesser Hampden are being re-laid in 2015 at the outdoor training facility at Crownpoint at Bridgeton in the city's East End and at the national competition venue of Grangemouth stadium in Falkirk.

Beyond the sporting venues

The public focus is, of course, on the main sporting venues where the action takes place and on the locations of the associated cultural festival activities. In Glasgow these were the three sporting venue clusters and the cultural festivities which occurred at Glasgow Green, Merchant City and Kelvingrove Park Live Zones, and the 'Pop up festival at the Quay' outside the BBC Scotland headquarters.

Did you know?
At the 2014 Games, events were held at three venues outside of the city - with shooting at the Ministry of Defence's training facility at Barry Buddon Shooting Centre at Carnoustie; the diving in the Royal Commonwealth Pool in Edinburgh; and the triathlon at Strathclyde Park, Motherwell.

Less obvious, but just as vital for the successful operation of an event like the Commonwealth Games, is the range of venues which are required for other reasons that provide essential support.

Firstly, there has to be accommodation for the thousands of athletes and officials who are the essential component of the Games. As this 'Athletes' Village' needs to be within a single campus or location, many host cities in the past have used student accommodation and others have built temporary housing. The approach in Glasgow was very different, seeing this as an opportunity to build homes for the future (see Chapter 4).

Second, there must be training venues enabling the athletes from across the Commonwealth to prepare when they are in the city. Some of this was accommodated in the Athletes' Village where a well-equipped fitness suite and gymnasium were provided. But for other sports, especially the team events, access to training spaces required more extensive facilities. Glasgow City Council provided these at

Toryglen Regional Football Centre, and Scotstoun Stadium. To meet the requirements of the nearly 4000 athletes, other training venues and facilities were required, and these were offered across Scotland by local authorities, such as the Dollan Aqua Centre in East Kilbride and the University of Stirling – either for national teams or for specific sports.

Third, and all too often forgotten at Games time, but central to the way that Glasgow approached the planning of the Games, there is the need to plan other venues where communities, groups and clubs displaced during Games time have a chance to continue their own sport and community activity. As Glasgow citizens were already using all the venues, there was a need for Glasgow Life and the other Council departments to organise alternative venues. Ensuring that they could stay active during the closure of the Sports Complex in the months around the Games, plans were made and communicated to users on alternative venues. These included the location of the other nineteen gyms open across the city, Glasgow Club facilities at Maryhill and Garscadden for fitness classes, and the opening of two Super Gyms in the Gorbals and Bellahouston in early 2014 to help provide suitable alternative facilities for Glaswegians.

Facilities too were required for the Glasgow 2014 workforce, for the volunteers, and for the logistics to support an event of this size. With a workforce reaching almost 1400 staff at its peak, the Organising Committee needed a dedicated office space in which it could expand during the planning period of the Games. With a budget of £7m allocated to spend on a headquarters, the OC were keen to refurbish George House on George Square. This occupied a prime site in the city centre and would have given high prominence to the OC's operations. However the property was privately owned and thus the investment in refurbishment would have been lost to the citizens of Glasgow. Reinforcing its desire to achieve a legacy wherever possible, Glasgow City Council were adamant that the money should be used to create a facility for the city after the Games. An empty property at Trongate and Albion Street owned by the Council but in need of upgrading so that it could be let thereafter was offered to the OC. Although not as central a location for the OC, the use of the money created an enhanced asset of a modern and high quality office space, labelled Commonwealth House. The space provided not only offices and meeting rooms, but was also the base for Clydesider interviews and formed the public face of the OC in the lead up to the Games.

And in the weeks leading up to the Games, space was needed to equip the 12,500 volunteer Clydesiders, to provide facilities for the buses, vans and cars to transport people and equipment between venues, and for the associated support services that help to keep the city moving. All of this requires considerable space and coordination. The Kelvin Hall was transformed into the Uniform and Accreditation Centre where the Clydesiders as well as the Games workforce and contractors picked up their uniforms and accreditation and security passes. The fleet of 1100 cars and vans provided by Ford under the Fleet Sponsorship Agreement with Glasgow 2014 was stored primarily at Arnold Clark's South Street depot where training and garaging facilities were available with smaller depots being used across the city during the Games. Other services such as the incident support on trunk roads provided by Scotland TranServ for Transport Scotland were expanded and operatives and vehicles located at strategic sites around the city.

Building on success

In contrast to previous host cities which often had to commit to major infrastructure programmes, the Council's history of investment in sporting and cultural facilities gave the opportunity to use the Games to build on its existing success and extend its pedigree as a sports city. For the Games itself, this past investment meant that there was less risk of cost overruns and non-completion. It also meant that the city had a wealth of local expertise available to help shape the bid, to work with the CGF and the Organising Committee, and to ensure that there would be a legacy from the event. As a result, unlike the established pattern where the OC leads on Games venue development, it was agreed that the City Council would lead on the design, development and construction of the infrastructure, with the OC contributing to the specification of the venues.

But even more crucial, it allowed those putting together the bid to place the 2014 Games into a wider context of Glasgow's ambitious plans for regeneration, and to incorporate the proven track record of the city in terms of hosting events, its passion for sport, and its drive to use sport to help improve wellbeing across the city.

Image 29:
Kelvingrove Art Gallery
& Museum with its
Floral Clyde

Image 30:
Sunny Evening at a
Packed Hampden Park

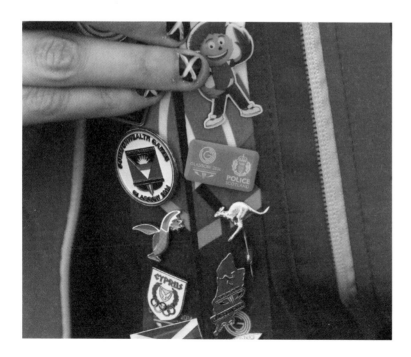

GLAS

"Not only does the bid provide the case to the CGF to be selected as host city but it also sets out the expectations of the Games and their impact on the city. It becomes the blueprint for the Games"

Chapter 3
Bidding for the Games, shaping expectations

Being selected as 'host city' for the Commonwealth Games marks a key stage in preparing for this major sporting event. In a formal sense it is the change from *a* 2014 candidate city to *the* host city, having convinced other national associations that the city is fit and able to be host. It also marks a transition from having a plan within the bid to getting to the starting line for the delivery of the Games themselves... and to seven years of further planning and preparation.

And whilst much of the public and media attention that accompanies the title of host city focusses on this next stage, the considerable effort put into the bidding process tends to be overlooked. Yet, arguably, the bid stage is the most important moment in the journey to the Games. Not only does the bid provide the case to the CGF to be selected as host city but it also sets out the expectations of the Games and their impact for the city. It becomes the blueprint for the Games and, if not thoroughly researched and robustly constructed, can create problems in the future.

The writing and development of the bid document is a major undertaking and for Glasgow was also a key moment in bringing together the city's sporting expertise, its aspirations for the future, and its ambitions for the Games themselves. Following a review of the procedures used by the CGF to select the host city for the Commonwealth Games, the bidding cities for 2014 were required to develop a much more extensive and exhaustive bid document than had been used previously. Developed by the same consultants that had developed the bid process for the International Olympic Committee, the 2014 process was more thorough and technically complex than for any previous Games.

The Glasgow bid

As the basis for the agreement signed between the CGF and the host city, the Candidate City File, to give the bid its formal title, has become a significant document. Glasgow's bid document – People, Place, Passion – was 251 pages setting out the case why the city believed it could and should host the Games. It was the result of considerable effort by the team of people assembled to meet the exacting requirements of the CGF, detailing not only why and how Glasgow could host the event, but also why the CGF could have confidence in those involved from Glasgow and Scotland that the Games would be delivered on time, on budget and to the standard that would be expected by the CGF.

Beyond the technical details – and there was a considerable amount of this – the Glasgow bid had at its heart a number of key elements which pointed to a low risk of venues not being available, relatively low costs to the Games which would be well managed to reduce risk of overspend, and for enormous public support guaranteeing high attendances at events. The bid expressed these in the following way:

- Glasgow has a strong track record in hosting sporting and cultural events and has much of the infrastructure required to host the Games. With 70% of the venues already built or planned, the remainder would be delivered well in advance of the Games

- Hosting the Games will provide a lasting legacy for the city, continuing to support its regeneration and, with unprecedented levels of public support, will provide a great celebration of sport

- There is a strong partnership approach to the delivery of the Games with clear leadership locally and nationally which will manage costs effectively

- The vision and ethos of the Commonwealth Games as a friendly, world class event is shared by Glasgow, and support will be provided to assist sports development for Commonwealth Games Associations and to support athletes and officials to attend.

Alongside this statement of passion for sport and the commitment of and to people, the rest of the bid document covered all the required technical and supporting information requested by the CGF.

Image 36:
Action from the Athletics
on Day Six

Image 37:
Shooting at the Barry
Budden Shooting
Centre, Carnoustie

Glasgow's Commonwealth Games: behind the scenes

Not only did the document have to present Glasgow's blueprint for organising the Commonwealth Games, it had to provide background information to help familiarise the CGF members with the city and the nation (see box).

The Candidate City File contents

	THEMES		MAX PAGES
VOLUME 1		Introduction	8
	Theme 1	Commonwealth Games Concept & Legacy	7
	Theme 2	Political and Economic Climate & Structure	7
	Theme 3	Legal Aspects	5
	Theme 4	Customs and Immigration Formalities	4
	Theme 5	Environment and Meteorology	13
	Theme 6	Finance	10
	Theme 7	Marketing	15
		Max	67
VOLUME 2		Introduction	3
	Theme 8	Sports and Venues	50
	Theme 9	Commonwealth Games Athletes' Village	25
		Max	78
VOLUME 3		Introduction	3
	Theme 10	Medical and Health Services	7
	Theme 11	Security	12
	Theme 12	Accommodation	25
	Theme 13	Transport	25
	Theme 14	Technology	7
	Theme 15	Media Operations	7
	Theme 16	Culture	7
		Conclusion	2
		Max	95
		TOTAL (MAX)	**240**

In addition, the CGF expected certain guarantees to be provided – committing the bidding city and nation to providing financial, legal, and other measures to support the delivery of the event if selected as host city. Some of these required new legislation to be passed – such as copyright and legal protection of 'Glasgow 2014', or the right of entry into the country of competitors and officials. This required agreement from the Scottish Parliament and from the UK Home Office. Other guarantees were financial, and needed the approval of a Games budget and underwriting to enable this to be offered in the bid document.

The complexity of the process meant that the bid team had not only to identify the operational plan for delivery of a successful Games but also had to liaise extensively with authorities across Scotland and the UK in order to put together the documentation to deliver the 40 areas of guarantees required by the CGF. These included financial support of the Games (underwritten by the Scottish Government), protection of the rights of association (under a special Act of Parliament), and securing the use of transport, other venues, hotel accommodation, security, medical services, immigration, technology, off-set of climate change and facilitation of media operations as well as minimising tax and visa restrictions for athletes such as Usain Bolt to be encouraged to attend the Games.

To achieve these requires a strong commitment from all those involved and a clear sense of responsibility. One of the defining dimensions of the bid process in Glasgow was the clarity over the roles of the City Council and the Scottish Government. Whilst the latter provided many of the required guarantees, including contributing 80% of the public sector costs, much more responsibility than in previous host city bids lay within the city. This reflected the City Council's larger organisational size and capacity, its own experiences in event management and delivery, and the fact that venues and other facilities were already owned by and managed for the Council. As a result, the Council took on leadership in areas such as venue delivery, transport, and legacy planning which other host cities have left the OC to organise.

Understandably, given the rigorous system put in place by the CGF for the first time for the 2014 Games, the process of bidding required to a greater degree than in past Games a huge commitment by many others beyond the bid team, including the business community in Glasgow (e.g. to guarantee the availability of hotel beds in 7 years' time) as well as demonstrating public support.

Being able to bid

As this bidding process illustrates, the decision to be considered as a candidate city for the Commonwealth Games is not one that can be taken quickly or lightly. After the set of 'what if' conversations in Manchester in 2002 described in Chapter 1, it took a further three years for the final decision to be reached that Glasgow would be put forward as a potential host city for the 2014 Games.

Initially the main potential contributors to any such bid within Scotland had to be convinced that hosting the Games in 2014 would be positive for Scotland. For any such bid to emerge, the Commonwealth Games Council for Scotland as the association representing the nation in the Commonwealth Games Federation would have to formally present the case. With both Louise Martin and Jon Doig from CGCS involved from the start, they led the discussions over several months. Although initially divided on the viability of a bid, the Board gradually moved towards offering their support and became strong advocates for Scotland.

At national government level, the discussions were led by the First Minister Jack McConnell. Recognising the considerable costs potentially associated with any bid and having to make judgements about the benefits for Scotland, one of the key foci of the discussions was on a bid which could be submitted without excessive public funding, but with the government's policy focus on linking sport and health, there were compelling reasons to support a bid.

Reassured of the potential merit of a making a bid, in 2004 a public announcement was made by the Commonwealth Games Council for Scotland on behalf of the Scottish Government asking for expressions of interest and plans from Scottish cities to be considered as a potential candidate for Scotland.

Meantime, there had been a parallel set of conversations being held in Glasgow City Council. The Cultural and Leisure Services team, later Glasgow Life, had also returned from Manchester considering how sport could be used to assist in the city's regeneration. As noted in the first chapter, the positive experience of the cultural regeneration strategy provided a blueprint for a similar sport strategy. Although this did not initially include the Commonwealth Games (at least not as early as 2014), the team in the Council had since Manchester 2002 been planning their sports infrastructure and investment strategy. They had scoped out the range of facilities which Glasgow as a city required to meet local needs and to enable it to compete for national and international events, and they had already sought to bid for opportunities under the Facilities Review. Informally as part of this process, the leadership team in the Council had signalled to the Scottish Government and CGS that they would be prepared to host the Commonwealth Games if supported.

The opportunity provided by the Scottish Government's announcement of Scotland's intention to bid was an ideal opportunity for this planning to be formalised and in 2004 they presented a bid to be Scotland's candidate city. Edinburgh also submitted a case, but in the resulting mini-competition there was overwhelming support for the Glasgow proposition.

In presenting their bid to CGS in Stirling in 2004, Glasgow had a strong twin focus - one that looked to sport to help the city in its wider regeneration, thus providing a strong case for public investment, and a second one on a commitment to high quality training and playing facilities to support elite support alongside community sport development, reinforcing the aims of SportScotland (and the CGS). And there was a commitment to using existing facilities, providing a realistic case to bid without very large public funding being required.

As Louise Martin and the CGS board indicated, the Glasgow bid "would have beaten any other country at previous Games. The document they submitted was absolutely fantastic". The unanimous decision of the CGS was to back Glasgow's bid and help to make a case for a formal bid.

Having crossed this first hurdle on the journey towards being host city, the City Council team still had to convince the Scottish Government that their case was worthy of public funding and support. Whilst key ministers were keen to advance a Scottish bid in Glasgow, the necessary expenditure of many millions of pounds required greater external and independent scrutiny and they felt the need for an assessment of whether a bid for 2014 might be premature and a bid for 2018 more realistic and likely to succeed. In addition, there was also the need to secure cross-party support within parliament for any bid.

The First Minister secured all party support for the bid which ensured that the Games were positioned outside of party politics and that, in 2007, the election of the Scottish National Party to government and Alex Salmond as First Minister did not reduce the commitment of the government to the Games. Two independent reviews of the Glasgow bid were commissioned by ministers, concluding that hosting the Games could bring positive economic and sporting benefits to Glasgow and Scotland. Reassured by this evidence, the Scottish Government gave the green light to become a full partner in the bid, an essential component of any successful bid.

Did you know?
The Sports Council of Great Britain was renamed UK
Sport in 1997 and is responsible for promoting and
supporting sport development. It is responsible for the
investment of National Lottery and government income
into Olympic and Paralympic sport. It works closely
with SportScotland, the national agency for sport.

Building the team

Having won this internal competition and with the support of the
Scottish Government in place to provide 80% of the public sector
funding, and with the support of the CGS, the City Council as lead
partner was by mid 2005 in a position to form a bid team to help take
forward the writing of the formal document... and to garner support
from other Commonwealth Games Associations to help the city win
the right to host the Games in 2014.

At the end of 2005, when progress on getting the bid together had
largely stalled, in a bold decision – and one that ran counter to the
approach adopted by most other candidate cities – the Glasgow team
decided not to set up an independent company to manage the bid but
to draw on expertise within the city and of the Scottish partners. The
decision not to introduce another party into the team to lead the bid
proved beneficial, if risky.

Instead Derek Casey was appointed as bid director in January
2006, in a role that coordinated the input from the City Council, Scottish Government and Commonwealth Games Scotland. Derek came
highly recommended and was familiar with the process of bidding
and international sports development– and had knowledge of key
people in the sports and cultural sector in Glasgow. He had been
director for the Sports Council of Great Britain and been involved in
sports programmes which delivered athletic success at the Beijing
Olympics in 2004. His leadership, knowledge and expertise were
crucial in giving the required momentum to the bidding process and
his extensive networks within the sporting community proved valuable in ensuring the bid not only fitted the local aspirations but has
aligned to the needs of the CGF and the different national sporting
bodies across the Commonwealth.

The decision to take control of the bid development locally allowed the partners to understand their responsibilities and to gain
confidence that they were able to work effectively together – creating
the foundations for the effective partnerships that helped deliver the

Games. Equally important was that this structure enabled staff to be added to the bid team from within the partner organisations – only two positions in the bid team were filled externally.

In part, however, this approach to developing a local bid team without the need to bring in external consultants was only possible and realistic because there was already considerable expertise in the city teams (especially in the sports and culture services areas that became Glasgow Life during the bidding process), and there was strong support from George Black and the senior officers to enable staff to be seconded from City Council roles into the bid team.

Assessing the competition

In the process of developing the bid, the Canadian and Nigerian Commonwealth Associations had signalled their intention to bid. Both of these nations were viewed within Glasgow and Scotland as potentially stronger contenders. There was a clear argument for the Games to go, for the first time, to an African nation and city. The experience of Kuala Lumpur in 1998 had been largely positive and underlined that countries without previous experience of being host were very capable of delivering a high-quality Games.

The case for holding the next Games in Canada was also strong. Experience from recent bidding processes to the Commonwealth Games Federation (CGF) was that cities bidding for the first time struggled to garner sufficient support from Federation members. In contrast cities re-bidding often put forward both a stronger case based on feedback from the CGF, and benefitted from greater levels of familiarity amongst voting members. In 2003 the decision by a narrow margin to award the 2010 Games to Delhi over Hamilton in Canada meant that there was concern in the Glasgow team that a bid from Hamilton for the 2014 Games would be a very strong contender.

When Canada announced that Halifax was their preferred candidate city, this concern was reduced and gave confidence that a Scottish bid could be a winning one. And with Abuja selected as the Nigerian candidate city, there was an acknowledgement that both it and Glasgow would be bidding for the first time.

Beyond this head-to-head competition there were other factors which might have militated against the Glasgow bid. The decision by the International Olympic Committee in 2005 to award the 2012 Summer Olympic and Paralympic Games to London had the potential to make another British bid less likely. And this was reinforced by the fact that Manchester (recently) and Edinburgh had already hosted the Commonwealth Games.

In responding to these circumstances, the Glasgow bid team sought to gain advantages.

First, they realised that in order to make a convincing argument for the Games to be attracted to Glasgow without any previous bidding history, they had to present a very robust technical bid which brought together the city's previous experience of hosting events.

Second, they had to emphasise that the city's investment in sporting and cultural infrastructure (Chapter 2) was an asset that could be used to help manage the overall cost of the event and ensure that costs associated with the Games would be maximised towards long term benefits rather than invested in new sporting venues. This was viewed as a strong response to the need for Halifax and Abuja to invest substantially in new facilities and venues.

Third, whilst there was understandable uncertainty about whether the decision to award the 2012 Summer Olympics to London would impact - positively or negatively - on federations, the Glasgow bid used the London success as a platform from which it could learn lessons quickly and be able to capitalise on these in the two years before the 2014 Games. The bid team's assessment was that overall there was a strong feeling that the London 2012 influence would be positive - an assessment which has been borne out!

Did you know?
Halifax in Canada withdrew its bid to be host city for the 2014 Commonwealth Games after the city was unable to gain support from the Canadian government to help underwrite the costs of the Games. Only two cities – Abuja in Nigeria and Glasgow – submitted bids.

Image 38:
The Fruitmarket in Glasgow receives the news

Image 39:
Glasgow schoolchildren celebrate the winning bid

Image 40:
Glasgow is awarded the 2014 Commonwealth Games

Glasgow's Commonwealth Games: behind the scenes

Image 41:
The 2014
Commonwealth Games
Host City is announced

Image 42:
The reaction at the
Glasgow Fruitmarket
as Glasgow is awarded
the Commonwealth
Games 2014

Glasgow's Commonwealth Games: behind the scenes

Putting together the Glasgow bid

Despite the expertise within the team of event delivery and of project management, the Glasgow bid team was largely unfamiliar with putting together a bid document of the complexity required by the CGF. Armed with the experience of the Manchester 2002 Games and the experience of bids from London and Manchester for the Olympics, Glasgow City Council and its two partners were able to draw on a wealth of previous experience to help shape its bid. In particular, the Manchester experience had underlined the importance of being ambitious whilst linking the Games into strategic priorities locally. In reflecting on the experience of putting together the Glasgow bid, those involved have underlined that they felt there were several key components that helped to convince each national association. First, listening to the requirements of the CGF – and thus providing a clear and robust bid document – and engaging each association in discussions about the vision and passion of the Glasgow bid was important to gain their support. In addition, building a strong coalition of interest behind the bid nationally and locally was crucial in demonstrating how the bid was aligned with existing strategies and visions for the city. And thirdly, having support from the public as well as the host city's elected representatives and officials, the national government and officials, the national representatives of the athletes and officials, and the athletes themselves all showed the depth of passion to be the host city.

In the first few months ahead of the Melbourne Commonwealth Games in March 2006 some progress had been made in the bid draft and an outline of the central themes was agreed. This was important in allowing the bid team and the partners led by the First Minister Jack McConnell to discuss the bid at the Melbourne Games. With the Scottish team having a strong performance in the Games, confidence was bolstered and there was an opportunity to get necessary constructive feedback on the emerging bid. The visit also allowed the bid team to gain crucial insights as part of the 'observer programme' at the Melbourne 2006 Games. But perhaps the most significant benefit was that the Games in Melbourne provided an opportunity for the first time to bring together all of the key people in the bid team and helped meld them into a strong unit.

Whilst a challenge to get the details required together, this process had many advantages for the bid team, not least because it meant that all the technical details associated with the delivery of the event had to work out, the funding sources needed to be identified, and decisions made about exactly which agency or partner would have responsibility for delivering each aspect.

Thinking imaginatively

Meeting the requirements of the CGF was not an easy task for the bid team, requiring them to explore imaginative and innovative ways to ensure that events such as shooting could be provided and the city could host track and field events without the need for new stadia.

Following the Dunblane massacre in 1996, the Scottish Government felt it was not able to support shooting as a sport in Scotland. Recognising that shooting was for some of the smaller territories and nations a key sport and that not to include it would lose the bid, the team explored the option of holding the shooting on the Isle of Man (not allowed by the CGF) and eventually agreed on hosting it within police or army grounds – successfully delivered at the Ministry of Defence shooting range at Carnoustie.

An even more imaginative solution had to be found to ensure that Glasgow could host track and field events within a large stadium. As the centre piece of the Games, attracting some of the largest crowds, greatest television coverage, and high-profile athletes, most host cities build such a stadium for the Games or have one built for previous events. The budget available in Glasgow did not allow for a new venue, and there were no suitably sized venues in Scotland. As noted above, the solution to adapt Hampden Park through the installation of a raised platform to provide the track was highly innovative.

Did you know?
The idea of inserting a platform track within an existing stadium had been proposed for Wembley Stadium at the design stage so that it could be used as part of a London Olympic bid. It was never realised as the overall capacity of the stadium would have been reduced too much. The Hampden Park Games track proved the feasibility of the idea – and it is likely to be copied in future by other cities.

By the time the bid was submitted there was, in effect, a well prepared operational plan with major issues thought out, key agencies identified, and actions proposed. The importance of learning from the recent experiences of host cities - Manchester in 2002 and Melbourne in 2006 - was expressed in terms of using these as 'benchmarks' against which the Glasgow bid could be placed. This helped both to inspire confidence in the development of the Games, but also underlined some of the differences which the Glasgow bid was proposing - for like all winning bids there needed to be some unique selling points to differentiate it from competitors.

At its heart the Glasgow bid had three main pillars:

- A low risk approach to providing venues with a commitment that 70% were already existing and most of the remainder were funded and planned, signalling the financial commitment from both the Glasgow City Council and Scottish government

- A clear sense of legacy for the city, aligned with the strategic aims of the city, placing the Games within a journey of social, environmental and economic renewal for Glasgow

- A celebration of the values of the Commonwealth, with support for and from communities across the city and nation and a development of the Games as a legacy.

Convincing the CGF

Persuading the CGF, and the national associations, that Glasgow would be a suitable host city involved more than submission of the bid document. Alongside the formal written bid document - the Candidate City File (CCF) - there was the need to provide formal submission and conduct reviews, and to host a visit from the technical committee of the CGF who provide a report on the feasibility of the bid presented. In addition, prospective host cities and nations lobby other nations to explain their vision and hope to persuade them of the merits of the bid - and, of course, win their vote!

Between the city's initial presentation of the Glasgow bid in Melbourne in 2006 and the formal written bid submitted to the CGF in May 2007, the bid team conducted visits to 66 Commonwealth

Image 44:

Track Cycling at the Sir
Chris Hoy Velodrome

Image 45:

Celebrating the
Commonwealth Games

Associations. In addition, opportunities were taken at sporting events across the world to meet with and discuss the emerging Glasgow plans. In total, 69 of the 71 Commonwealth nations were visited or had presentations from the Glasgow bid team, enabling the vision of a Glasgow Games to be shared and feedback from nations to be drawn upon in writing the final bid. These visits were also supported by a programme of inward visits to Glasgow/ Scotland with presentations, venue tours, hospitality and formal and informal events.

Although an expensive and time-consuming element, this approach to lobbying was viewed as an important part of the bid development process. For the bid team it allowed them to present their plans and hold discussions which shaped the way the city's plans could connect with other nations. It also enabled the team to work through remaining issues – some technical but most relating to the needs and priorities of each of the associations and their athletes. Once again the commitment of the leaders from the City Council and the Scottish Government to be part of some of these visits, and to enable key staff to attend the visits, was vital.

Did you know?
Between March 2006 and September 2007, the bid team attended Melbourne 2006 Commonwealth Games, Central American and Caribbean Games in Colombia, Asian Games in Doha, Pan American Games in Brazil, and the South Pacific Games in Samoa.

In return it also allowed other staff beyond the bid team to become more familiar with aspects of the bid and this assisted in enabling the plans to be implemented once Glasgow was announced as host city for 2014.

Getting the decision

In the decision making process the key inspection, following the CCF submission, was held in June 2007. Then the CGF Evaluation Commission, the body charged to assess the technical merits of each CCF, visited Glasgow to inspect the proposed venues, facilities and sites, and to interrogate the plans further.

The Commission's findings on the two bids were released in September 2007, with them underlining the 'thoughtful and practical approach' which had been taken by Glasgow to its bid and to the proposed Games. Its overall assessment was that "Glasgow has demonstrated an understanding of the major requirements to stage the Commonwealth Games". Most reassuring however was the acknowledgement made by the Commission that the venue and legacy issues were considered appropriately alongside the city's long-term needs.

The confidence of the Commission in the quality and standard of the bid was key in helping Glasgow win the right to be host city. Not only did it have an influence on the individual federations in their decision on which city to choose, but it reinforced the sense within the Glasgow bid team that their approach to ensuring a legacy for the Commonwealth Games and for the city was the right message.

The bid struck the right note between acknowledging the needs of the CGF and the Commonwealth Games as an event of athletic competition, and the desire and needs of Glasgow. In arguing that Glasgow wanted the Games to help the city on its journey of change, the bid also advocated change for the Games - making it more relevant and strongly connected with legacies that outlasted the 11 days of sport. The bid team was determined that the Games would not be an expensive spectacle which left white elephants and some memories, but no lasting benefits. Its bid - People, Place, Passion - reflected these goals and the Games which were delivered reflected all three components.

In Sri Lanka on 9th June 2007, ahead of the final decision, Louise Martin (chair of CGS), along with Alex Salmond (First Minister), and Steven Purcell (Leader of the Council) led the team for the final presentation. This selection of key people was deliberate, reinforcing the partnership of the CGS, Scottish Government and City Council, and was strengthened by the inclusion of Jamie Quarry, who had won Scotland's first decathlete medal in Manchester in 2002, to show the support from athletes. Three films highlighting the themes - the pride and passion of Glasgow, and the place showing venues and the Athletes' Village - reinforced the speeches. Together they signalled the desire of Glasgow and Scotland to host the 2014 Games.

And 46 other associations agreed, with the Glasgow case winning over that presented on behalf of Abuja in Nigeria.

The celebrations which accompanied this decision - in Glasgow, across Scotland and indeed internationally - underlined the value of the bid having won support from the citizens and businesses of Glasgow, having all party political support from the Scottish Government, showing a unity of passion and purpose that continued from the bid through to the Games in 2014.

"Glasgow City Council set out with an ambitious plan to use the Games to take the city further and faster along a development path to meet some of its strategic priorities"

Chapter 4
The People's Games
– meeting local needs

At the closing ceremony of the 2014 Games, the President of the CGF Prince Imran in his closing speech suggested that Glasgow had not only delivered the Friendly Games but "had succeeded in making them even more than that. These had truly been the People's Games".

While this comment reflected the enormous support and contribution made by the people of the city in general, there were other respects in which the Glasgow Games were trying to be the 'people's games'. In particular there was a strong drive within the City Council and their partners to ensure that the 2014 Games investment was an opportunity for Glasgow and Scottish companies and for people in Glasgow to feel the difference. Improving 'employment readiness' as well as 'business readiness' were some of the key aims of a range of support projects put in place.

Spending a budget of over £570m on a 12-day event celebrating sports and culture is not an easy decision, especially at a time when there are unprecedented pressures on public sector funding and many families across Glasgow, Scotland, and the Commonwealth are struggling on a daily basis to make ends meet. Not everyone was convinced that the hosting of the Games was the best use of public funds, and those involved in planning the Glasgow 2014 event have been conscious that every pound needed to count.

From the development of the bid, the City Council sought to ensure that the Glasgow Games were a means to help meet the needs of local communities. Recognising from the experience of Manchester in 2002 in particular that being host city provides a unique opportunity to 'mobilise' resources within the city and to capture new resources from beyond, GCC set out with an ambitious plan to use the Games to take the city further and faster along a development path to meet some of its strategic priorities.

The evidence from previous Games, however, suggested that

actually making a difference to communities was challenging. The lack of measurable evidence of impact on health and physical activity levels arising from being a host city was a reminder that other cities had also tried without any evidence of success to meet their similar local needs. In attempting to give a strong focus on ensuring benefits, the approach by the City Council and Scottish Government was made up of three key ingredients. First, there was a geographical focus on the East End of Glasgow, where by virtue of the concentration of investment on the Emirates Arena and Athletes' Village, were inevitably the most visible signs of meeting local needs. These two venues formed part of a larger and longer plan for regeneration, announced in 2007 as the remit of the Clyde Gateway Urban Regeneration Company.

Second, and primarily led by the City Council, was a strong desire to reach out to people in communities across the city that were struggling to get into the labour market. Initiatives were set up to ensure that targeted groups could gain benefit from the expenditure on Games contracts and the employment opportunities available. Companies were encouraged and supported to provide a 'helping hand' to recruit those unemployed or lacking skills, providing them with opportunities to gain valuable skills and work experience.

And third, learning from the experience of previous major events, and in particular London 2012, support was offered to help local businesses to be better positioned to win a share of the contracts available associated with the Games – and then other public sector contracts.

The East End Gateway

Some of the most potent symbols that the Games have had an impact on local communities lie in the Dalmarnock area of the city, site of the Emirates Arena and the Athletes' Village as well as close to Parkhead Stadium where the Games opened. It has been the part of the city that has been most transformed physically by the Games preparation and investment and one that has caught the media attention.

The process of change within the area had already started years in advance of the decision to bid for the Games but, when the Council was looking for a suitable site for the Games Athletes' Village, the area of Dalmarnock was identified as both a vacant site and one that could gain greatest benefit from Games expenditure. The area bore the scars of previous phases of planned but incomplete renewal with pockets of vacant land between Victorian or Edwardian tenements and the 1950s and 1960s housing developments. The City Council had already earmarked the area for renewal, had demolished some of the high rise blocks of flats at the start of the 21st century, and planned the demolition of the remainder. Physically the landscape portrayed the population decline in the area and the lack of investment over decades.

However appearances can be deceptive. Despite the declining community facilities in the area – including school, surgery, local shops – Dalmarnock also has a strong sense of community, with many families having lived in the area for several generations, and bound together partly in shared adversity and partly from their strong roots in the area. Building on this heritage and continuing pride, but also seeking to address the long-term lack of investment in the area, the Clyde Gateway Urban Regeneration Company was set up in December 2007. Extending over an area of 840 hectares (2000 acres), the partnership involves Glasgow City and South Lanarkshire Councils as well as Scottish Enterprise and is backed by funding from the Scottish Government. With a 20 year programme of investment, Clyde Gateway is seeking to transform the area.

Whilst the investment in the area as part of the Commonwealth Games has been both a major and visible sign of the changing approach to regeneration in the area and a catalyst for attracting other investment, success will be as much about social and economic transformations in the lives of the local communities as the physical landscape.

Reclaiming land

The development of the Athletes' Village site provided an opportunity not only to generate a new housing facility for the Games and thereafter, but also a chance to return some of the contaminated and derelict land into use. One of the reasons for the lack of previous investment and regeneration in the area was the large amount of possible soil contamination. As the site of former foundries and industrial works, much of it related to the heavy industry and shipbuilding elsewhere in the city, and made famous for its structural engineering contributions to the building of the Forth Rail bridge, waste and residues from the works had percolated into the soil. The cost of decontamination had hampered previous attempts to bring the area back into productive use but the development of the Athletes' Village provided the opportunity for the City Council to take the initiative to help stimulate housing development in the area and manage the process of land reclamation.

Did you know?
Of the 38.5 hectares involved in the site development
for the Games, 33 hectares required soil remediation.
Specialist soil washing contractors were appointed to
allow this to occur without the need for removing the
soil to landfill.

The process of acquiring land and 'cleaning' it has not been without
controversy or challenge. The use of a compulsory purchase order to
complete the demolition of homes and shops in the area raised concerns about the 'shared vision' of the Games as some displacement of
businesses had to take place. And more difficult was that the fact that
the City Council and Clyde Gateway did not own all the land needed for
the village. To meet its bid commitments and acquire the necessary
land, the City Council has had to broker deals with local landowners.
Some plots had been lying vacant for as much as 20 years, with limited potential for development linked to contamination. Others had
been sold off to developers only a few years previously. With the need
to broker separate deals, there has been concern about the high costs
to the Council in acquiring the land with some developers seeing land
values more than doubling over a couple of years.

As a result there was a delay before the process of development and
decontamination could start. With the City Council leading on the
development of the site for the Athletes' Village, tenders were invited
from organisations to undertake the project – with the desire to meet
the Council's aim of bringing the area back into community use. The
winning bid was from a consortium, City Legacy, created specially to
develop the Athletes' Village site. The team brought together experts
in land development and housing construction from Scottish based
companies WH Malcolm, Mactaggart & Mickel, Cruden Homes and
CCG. Their plan not only saw the village as a future community but
one that also met the highest standards for environmental sustainability.

Image 47:
The Site of the
Athletes' Village Before
Regeneration, Glasgow's
East End

Image 48:
Councillor George
Redmond outside his
old house in Ardenlea
Street, Dalmarnock

Glasgow's Commonwealth Games: behind the scenes

Glasgow's Commonwealth Games: behind the scenes

The Athletes' Village: a new East End community

The Athletes' Village housing development is designed to breathe
new life into an area where decline has been the main trajectory for a
generation. Along with the wider economic regeneration programme
of the Clyde Gateway project, the expectation is that the Games will
cast a new spotlight on the potential of the area and encourage further investment.

For the athletes taking part in the Commonwealth Games, the
village adjacent to the Emirates was a big hit. For those who had experienced accommodation in Delhi and in London, the open space
– houses (rather than large apartment blocks) – and the village feel
made it a great centre for them. As one athlete told me, "it was like
being at home".

And that is exactly what the village is aiming to be. The formation
of home zones streets, waterside steadings, car free areas, floodable
landscapes of canals and ponds between the houses is designed to redefine the image and living environment of the East End of Glasgow.
As City Legacy, the partnership responsible for the creation of the village, indicate in their marketing, this is the 'New East End'. The properties have been designed and constructed to the highest energy efficiency and sustainability standards. The central heating plant at the
Energy Centre – the first in Glasgow – supplies all the houses as well as
the Emirates Arena with hot water, heating and power, offering much
lower bills for homeowners. This is augmented by solar roof panels.

In the months leading up to the start of the Games when the village
homes were showcased and pre-bookings were being taken, public
interest was high and the majority of properties had already secured
new home owners.

Under the arrangements made by the City Council with City Legacy, 400 of the 700 homes were made available at affordable rent and
the remainder sold privately. A mixed community has been created
with a range of 1 to 4 bedroom apartments, townhouse and detached
properties across the site as well as a care home. The rented houses

will be managed through three housing associations - Glasgow Housing, Thenue Housing and West of Scotland - with the City Council's Social Services department managing the care home. The second phase in 2015 will see further homes being built on the northern part of the site, and a new bridge across the Clyde connecting to the Cuningar Loop woodland park. This parkland - itself a derelict site - is being transformed into a community resource as a legacy project from the Commonwealth Games.

Did you know?
As part of the innovative design of the houses which made up the Athletes' Village, the building consortium City Legacy developed off-site fabrication methods which allowed a single townhouse to be constructed in only 10 days. This process is now being used in other housing projects in the city.

Associated with the development a highly sustainable build, the Dalmarnock village development has included the city's first district heating network. The possible use of district heating schemes across the city to offer cheaper heating and power had been a main element of the Sustainable Glasgow Initiative report published in 2012. The Athletes' Village development offers not only 40% greater efficiency in supply but much lower bills for households, estimated to be a saving of £500 each year, and the technology used here offers the opportunity to be replicated in future developments across the city as well as offering the opportunity to address some of the fuel poverty issues felt by residents.

Integrating communities
The creation of a 'new East End' however also presents challenges not least in integrating this into the existing community. In the past, regeneration projects have often been 'done to' people in the area rather than 'done with' them and there has been considerable scepticism that local residents will see the benefits from the Games venues.

This was epitomised by the debate over creating a new, fit for purpose community centre in Dalmarnock. Although a new community hub is now being built, this has only been achieved with some considerable effort by the local residents and several 'false starts'. When plans for the Athletes' Village were originally being drawn up, pressure was put on the City Council and partners by local residents to design a facility that could be retrofitted into a new community centre. They argued for the temporary catering centre at Games time to be made into a permanent resource. However, operational difficulties made this impossible for the OC and alternative plans were considered by the Council and the local community. When plans were announced for the closure and demolition of the existing community centre at the end of 2013 to make space for temporary Games time activity, pressure from the local community mounted for them to have a new facility.

After months of negotiation and the mobilisation of local people to get involved with the programme of regeneration in the area, a solution was found. The City Council sold land adjacent to the Emirates Arena for £1 to the newly formed local Dalmarnock's People's Development Trust who will take on the financial responsibility of managing the centre. The cost of the new centre is being met by funding from the Big Lottery Fund, the City Council and the Scottish Government, with the new centre helping to generate income to meet operating costs and offset some of the capital costs.

Opening in 2015 the new hub will provide an all-purpose community hall, nursery, GP surgery, pharmacy, convenience store and café. It will also create 60 new jobs, including those associated with the new nursery, and will help to service the needs of the new community at Dalmarnock, as the Athletes' village started to be occupied in early 2015.

Led by enthusiastic and committed individuals from the community, most noticeably recently elected Councillor Yvonne Kucuk, the Development Trust has also helped with the support of the Velocity Public Art Commission to create a new adventure playground on a derelict site in Baltic Street, and is taking forward plans for a community shop.

Getting active
Connecting the Dalmarnock and East End communities with the legacy aims of the Games has extended beyond these new facilities. Recognising the separation of the area from other parts of the city, new roads, pathways and cycleways have been created in a network across the city designed to help reconnect the East End with the city as a whole as well as helping to move people during the Games (see Chapter 7).

The opening of the Clyde Gateway road for example is a key part of the regeneration plan for the area, connecting the new M74 southern extension with the M80 to the north. It has opened up the area for future investment, including the new Police Scotland offices at Riverside East opening early in 2015. Cycleways and footpaths have been created that criss-cross the old street patterns of the Dalmarnock and Bridgeton areas. The cycle paths help to reconnect the 10.5 mile Clyde Walkway route to the communities and facilities in the area, and form a key component of the 200km long network of cycle routes across the city. And they will enable local residents to be a leading part of the initiative to make 'Glasgow more active'.

Did you know?
The increase in cycling within Glasgow has led to an expansion of online websites offering information about routes and capturing users' views on each route. The apps include the Glasgow Cycling app provided free on the Future City Glasgow's open data website

These physical changes have been reinforced by the City Council's cycling strategy which has not only taken a more strategic approach to planning for cycling, but has also helped support local cycle proficiency training, school bike loan schemes, and cycling promotional activity such as European Mobility Week, Bike Week and the Pedal for Scotland Event.

Evidence from the communities of the East End of the city conducted as part of the GoWell East legacy research study points to cycling rates – both for commuting and recreation – being higher in the city as a whole with 5% of those in employment cycling to work or study, and overall 1 in 7 cycling in the last month when asked. With positive feedback from local communities on the improvements in pathways and lighting, there is also evidence that this might help address the low levels of walking – with as many as 2 in 5 not walking for at least 20 minutes during a week.

Helping Glaswegians into employment
The desire to ensure that the Games had a longer lasting impact on the economy of Glasgow was a key driver for much of the activity of the Council and its partners. Not only did this help to justify the public

Image 50:
Support For the
Commonwealth Games

Image 51:
Crowds Gathering in the
Sun to Watch the Games,
Glasgow Green

Image 52:
Environmental
improvements at
Dalmarnock

Image 53:
Empire Café event
in the Briggait

expenditure associated with the event but it was also a key means of ensuring support from the local business community. Although Glasgow's economy has changed significantly in the last few decades to embrace more retail and financial services, there remains an important manufacturing and construction sector. However, in this post-industrial change the city has also suffered from relatively high and persistent unemployment. For the City Council the developments required to meet the needs of the Commonwealth Games were also an opportunity to generate a springboard for businesses and citizens.

Did you know?
Community benefit clauses can be included into public contracts as long as they do not contravene EU procurement rules. Glasgow City Council has been proactive in including community benefit clauses, particularly focusing on recruitment and training, developing supply chains, and developing social enterprises. The clauses were included in the programme to develop infrastructure for the 2014 Commonwealth Games.

This ambition was expressed within one of the legacies from the Games – that of a prosperous Glasgow. Under this theme, action has focused on ensuring investment in infrastructure, services and functions connected directly to the event has longer benefits for the city in its continuing progress towards a modern, mixed economic base. This has meant the Council and its partners have sought to provide as many opportunities for people in Glasgow who are currently outside of employment – those leaving school, those unemployed and those leaving training and university – as possible. Initiatives targeted at each of these groups were set up well ahead of the Commonwealth Games. Action was taken by the Council with support from government to ensure that all the contracts awarded in connection with the Games – the construction of the new venues, infrastructural projects, and in the services required for the event – provided opportunities for those furthest from the labour market in terms of skills and experience. In addition, assistance and support was provided to employers to win these contracts as well as other projects being offered by the Council through public procurement.

Together this focus has been on helping build a skilled and motivated workforce across the city, reaching into communities and areas which struggled during the global economic crisis and where families and individuals have faced long periods out of work.

A series of measures – the Commonwealth Employment Initiatives – was put in place by the City Council with support from other agencies to assist these groups. With employment rates in Glasgow being 8% below the Scottish average and with as many as 30% of households in the city having no adult in employment, also higher than the national average, these schemes have made a small but significant contribution to the issue of economic participation. Alongside the contribution made through the volunteering experiences (discussed in Chapter 8), this has helped Glaswegians to build their confidence and gain important skills.

These initiatives sought to target key groups of people within Glasgow – either because they needed assistance to enter (or re-enter) the workforce or were viewed as key groups to the future economic strategic development of the city. Most of the schemes involved financial support being provided to employers to recruit new staff or offer new positions. Some of these were directly linked to Games' projects but most were not, seeking to ensure that the benefits were felt more widely across the city's communities.

The first and largest scheme was the Commonwealth Apprenticeship Initiative created with the aim of taking suitably qualified school leavers in the city into workplace opportunities as apprentices for a period of 2 to 4 years. Financial support of up to £4000 per person was provided for half the duration of the apprenticeship as well as assistance in the recruitment process. Under the scheme each young person not only gained valuable work experience but was provided with the opportunity to gain a qualification, either through part-time college course enrolment or by working towards SVQ level 2 or 3 in the workplace. For those who have struggled to get into work either being unemployed or on leaving education have been supported by the Commonwealth Jobs Fund, the Commonwealth Youth Fund or through the New Entrant Trainees scheme. This Trainee scheme was designed to target the long-term unemployed, offering a mix of work on Games-related infrastructure projects or as apprentices.

Did you know?
The success of the Commonwealth Apprenticeship Initiative has meant that the scheme's life has been extended to at least 2017.

For young people leaving university in the city, the Commonwealth Graduate Fund has been designed to retain talent in the city, with over 680 graduates assisted by the scheme. The fund links with the city's economic strategy requiring a higher skilled labour pool in key sectors and signals a renewed focus on capturing the considerable pool of graduate talent that is generated by the universities and colleges in the city. Each year approximately 8300 students graduate from the city's three universities, with students contributing as one of the main economic groups to the city's economic base.

Did you know?
Under the employment schemes, nearly 5,500 Glaswegians have been helped into employment – under the Commonwealth Apprenticeship Initiative (3,294), the Commonwealth Jobs Fund (790), the Commonwealth Graduate Fund (666), the New Entrant Trainees (500) and the Commonwealth Youth Fund (243).

Across this range of initiatives, significant impacts have been made to help address the long-term goal of increasing levels of employment and skill levels in the city, and have set a model for future public sector contracts.

Using the local workforce

For those already in employment, the Commonwealth Games also provided a unique opportunity to gain additional experience and expertise. Many of the Clydesiders as well as the other volunteer groups viewed the Games as a potential opportunity to gain new skills and to use the ones they had. But for the City Council and its partners in Glasgow, the Games also created opportunities for some staff to learn firsthand skills that were important to their day jobs.

This was particularly true for staff from Glasgow Life. One consequence of the use of existing and newly opened venues as the location of the sporting events for the Commonwealth Games was that Glasgow already had an existing and knowledgeable workforce present at each site. In contrast, for example to many of the venues for the Delhi 2010 Games or the London 2012 Olympics where the OC had to train a workforce to operate in the new venues, Glasgow Life employees were already trained and operating at most sites.

This unique position for all venues provided an opportunity to capitalise on one of the lessons learnt from Manchester 2002, where the post-Games evaluation suggested that to provide a legacy for sport there was a need for greater support to staff to help with the delivery of the Games. Glasgow Life took this to heart and at Games time many of its staff in venues were involved with the OC, assisting them with local knowledge on venues and learning in return dimensions to help in the future use of the venues for events etc.

At the Emirates Arena, for example, most of the staff were given opportunities in the weeks leading up to the Games to become seconded into the OC workforce at the venue. For some, this gave the chance to focus on one aspect of their existing roles and to work towards a specific project and outcome. For others there was an opportunity to experience more responsibility or senior positions, working alongside external contractors who made the venue ready for the Games or with specialists in the OC.

With the OC under immense time pressure and with timescales slipping, the local knowledge and expertise was invaluable. It avoided the need to train additional staff, especially when in the lead up to the Games some of the team leaders in the OC left, taking with them knowledge about the plans and functioning of the venue. And having local staff available provided both knowledge and stability, as well as helping to make connections between the users of the building and the Games.

And for the staff and the Council family organisations, it has helped to gain knowledge from the Games that can be transferred to future events, and provided a sense of pride amongst the workforce and in the venues. They have had opportunities to step outside their normal roles and see other ways of working, new ideas, to gain skills and probably for some set new personal horizons. How the City Council and its agencies capitalise on this remains to be seen. Some staff will no doubt leave to fulfil the ambitions set by their experiences as part of Glasgow's Commonwealth Games. Others will help organise better future events, help set new standards of service and move their organisations forward. For all those involved – like many of the volunteers and others who for a fortnight became part of the Games – they are unlikely to return to their roles untouched by the experience.

Helping local businesses

Drawing on the experience of the London 2012 Olympics, the City Council and the Scottish Government developed ways in which businesses could be assisted to be better placed to gain some of the investment being made in Games venues and the associated infrastructure projects. Learning from the recent experience at the London 2012 Olympics, schemes were devised to enable local businesses to have greater knowledge of and opportunity to tender for the thousands of contracts and sub-contracts that were available with the Games.

Associated with the London Olympics, a scheme entitled CompeteFor was launched in January 2008. This provided free brokerage services, helping to match buyers (usually large companies) with potential suppliers. The focus of the scheme was on the sub-contracted (Tier 2 and 3) business, with an electronic brokerage system, and information and engagement programmes being used to link suppliers with the main contract holders. The scope of the CompeteFor service included other public procurement contracts in London and not just those directly linked to the Olympics. This scheme was viewed as beneficial for local companies in and around London, but had much less impact elsewhere across the UK.

Learning from the CompeteFor experience, in Glasgow the desire was to offer greater support to enable companies to be better positioned to win contracts. In particular there was a realisation that small or medium sized enterprises (SMEs) might not have the capacity to win contracts available around the Games – or more widely through public procurement – and few of them would be known to large contractors.

The Commonwealth Games Business Portal was created by the City Council to help provide more direct support for and build the capacity of local businesses. In addition to being a central register of companies interested in and capable of delivering aspects of the Commonwealth Games contracts and to provide an alert system of available contract, the Portal included a training component. This training focused on building capacity within small and medium sized companies to be in a stronger position to compete in future. This development of 'business readiness' was thus viewed as a desirable way of helping companies to get in place the requirements necessary to be matched with opportunities in advance of the contracts being released. The training included helping them to collect information on factors such as health and safety, equality and race relations, and to provide training to complete the public procurement tendering processes.

The success of the Business Portal scheme – more than 22,000 companies are now registered – has meant that the City Council and partners have extended the Portal to include both public and private sector contracts, and have made this apply to opportunities beyond the Commonwealth Games. Renamed the Glasgow Business Portal to reflect this wider remit, a commitment was made for it to continue to operate until at least 2017; although, in 2015, the scheme will be extended to a national one, merged with the Scottish Government's national procurement portal, Public Contracts Scotland. It now includes companies from across all Scottish local council areas as well as businesses from outside of Scotland.

At the national level, businesses were supported by the Scottish Government through the development of a scheme called Business Club Scotland. Managed by Scottish Enterprise, the club was launched in January 2009. It was designed to help Scottish business to capitalise on the opportunities for events in 2014, including the Commonwealth Games, Ryder Cup and Homecoming Scotland, enabling companies to build supply chain networks and to help raise awareness of the procurement opportunities associated with the Games.

Generating business and economic value

"The Commonwealth Games has helped to keep the city moving through a difficult economic period" was the opening message in the Legacy 2014 report released by Glasgow City Council just before the start of the Games. With clear evidence that a significant amount - almost 50% of the total value - of the investment made for the preparation of the Games went through contracts to local companies, and with new opportunities being created for young people in apprenticeships and Community Benefit Clauses - creating more than 5500 opportunities - the Games has helped to offset some of the economic challenges of the global economic downturn since 2008.

Beyond the public sector investment in Games related areas, Glasgow has also benefitted from private sector investment associated with being host city. Despite the drop in land values and construction, new hotels and accommodation in the city has been secured and some delivered in time for the Games. The city has seen major investment in hotel capacity stimulated not only by the need during the Games but through the accompanying growth in national and international tourism. Games time hotel developments have included investment by major chains such as De Vere Village, Premier Inn, Travelodge, Motel One, and Hampton Inn by Hilton as well as new developments such as Z-Hotel's redevelopment of the Old Printworks in John Street. Collectively these will add nearly 1,000 new hotel rooms to the city's accommodation stock by 2015.

The Games themselves generated some of the highest occupancy rates the city has ever seen. As early as the start of 2014, it was clear that occupancy rates were likely to reach record levels. Across the 11 nights of the Commonwealth Games (July 23 to August 3), Glasgow's hotels achieved average occupancy of 95.3%, reflecting an 11.2% increase on the same period in 2013. In addition, other parts of Scotland benefitted from the 'ripple effect' as travellers sought out alternative accommodation in other locations - especially in Dundee, Stirling and Edinburgh with easy connections by train to Glasgow. With high street sales increased by more than 10%, shopper numbers rising as much as 36%, record July numbers of passengers at Glasgow Airport (840,000), the immediate impact on the city's commercial sector was positive.

Importantly the Games in Glasgow also assisted business as usual – with the city animated and engaging, including at other sights and places. Visitor numbers, for example, at the city's museums rose during the Games, the opposite of the experience in London during the 2012 Olympics when other visitor attractions suffered a decline in numbers.

Did you know?
At Glasgow Green as part of the Live Zone, the Scottish Food Village provided an opportunity for 23 companies to showcase the best of Scottish food and celebrate the way that cultures from across the Commonwealth had influenced Scottish food. Each stall throughout the 12 days of the 2014 Festival served up thousands of portions of meat, seafood, puddings, juice and fruit from across Scotland.

Whilst the analysts decide on the final value to the city and Scotland, Glasgow City Marketing Bureau already knows that £200m worth of conferences have been attracted to the city in the next decade, attracted in part by the Commonwealth Games. With the SSE Hydro and the Emirates Arena as flagship venues, the rest of the city's sport and culture locations are also benefitting. And as this is just for business already secured by the end of the Games, there is confidence that even more economic benefits for the city's economy will come.

Image 54:

National Hockey Centre,
Glasgow Green

Image 55:

Cheering the Women's
Cycle Road Race,
Glasgow Green

Glasgow's Commonwealth Games: behind the scenes

Glasgow's Commonwealth Games: behind the scenes

Image 56:
John Barrowman
Performs During
The Glasgow 2014
Commonwealth Games
Opening Ceremony,
Celtic Park

Image 57:
HRH Queen Elizabeth
II Officially Opens
the Glasgow 2014
Commonwealth Games
Opening Ceremony,
Celtic Park

Image 58:
The Glasgow 2014
Commonwealth Games
Closing Ceremony,
Hampden Park

Image 59 :
The Glasgow 2014
Commonwealth Games
Closing Ceremony,
Hampden Park

Glasgow's Commonwealth Games: behind the scenes

MEN'S SINGLES   GOLD ME
        COURT GL

*MATTHEW M.   <ENG> 1

  11 8 3
   9 11 4

WILLSTROP   <ENG> 1

LONGINES

Ford

Ford

Image 60:
Scotstoun National
Squash Centre

Image 61:
Opening the Games,
Celtic Park

Image 64:
Kenya's Caleb
Mwangangi Ndiku at the
5000m, Hampden Park

Image 65:
5000m, Hampden Park

Image 66:
Weight Lifting, SECC

Image 69:
Women's Hockey,
National Hockey Centre

Image 70:
Support for Team
Scotland

Glasgow's Commonwealth Games: behind the scenes

Glasgow's Commonwealth Games: behind the scenes

Image 72:
Boxing

Image 73:
Artistic Gymnastics
Finals, The SSE Hydro
Glasgow 2014

Glasgow's Commonwealth Games: behind the scenes

Image 74:
Scotland's Josh Taylor
Celebrates his Win over
Kagiso Bagwasi from
Botswana in the Boxing

Image 75:
Women's Gymnastics

Image 76:
Closing Ceremony,
Hampden Park

Image 77:
Closing Ceremony,
Hampden Park

Glasgow's Commonwealth Games: behind the scenes

Image 78:
Fireworks at the Closing
Ceremony

Image 79:
Opening Ceremony
Scottie Dog

Glasgow's Commonwealth Games: behind the scenes

Glasgow's Commonwealth Games: behind the scenes

FAMILY ST
EXIT 4
SECOND HALF
ENG 15 - 12 SCO 2:25
EXIT 4
GLASGOW 2014
LONGINES

Image 82:
Rugby 7s Ibrox

Image 03.
Alistair Brownlee
Crosses the Line to win
the Mixed Relay Triathlon
for England, Strathclyde
Country Park

Image 84:
Swimming, Tollcross
International Swimming
Centre

Image 85:
Men's Singles Gold
Medal Match as
Scotland's Darren
Burnett Takes on Ryan
Bester of Canada,
Kelvingrove Lawn Bowls
Centre

Glasgow's Commonwealth Games: behind the scenes

Image 89:
Jennifer Abel of
Canada in the Women's
3m Springboard
Preliminaries, Royal
Commonwealth Pool

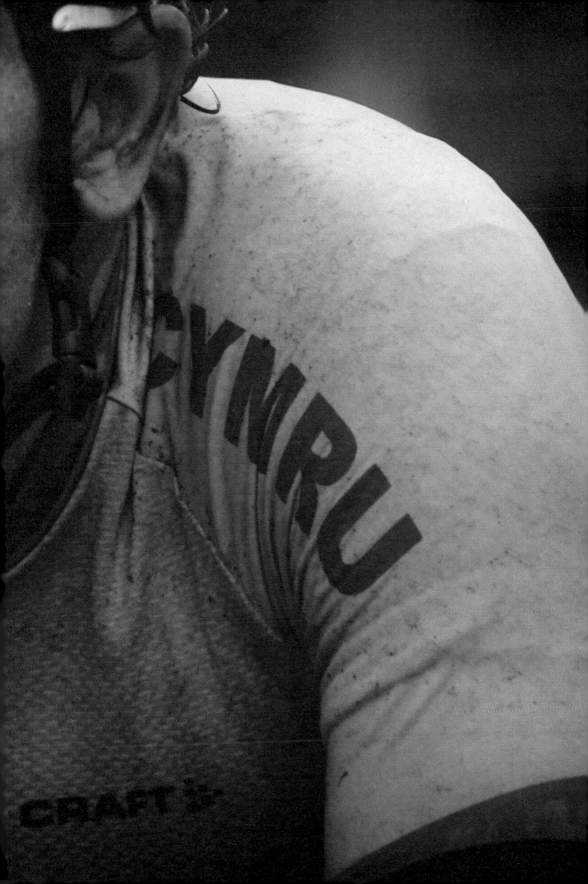

Image 90:
Geraint Thomas from
Wales wins the men's
cycling road race

Image 91:
Kah Mun Tong from
Singapore takes part in
the Gymnastics Rhythmic,
at the SECC Hydro

Image 92:
Crowds at Tollcross
Intentional Swimming
Centre

Image 93:
South Africa celebrate at
the final whistle against
New Zealand in the
Rugby 7s

Glasgow's Commonwealth Games: behind the scenes

Image 94:
Scotland's Robbie Renwick misses out on a medal in the Men's 200m Freestyle Final

Image 95:
Mark Dry of Team Scotland with his bronze medal for the Men's Hammer Throw

Image 96:
Malaysia win the gold medal against England in Badminton

Image 97:
Men's Double Trap Gold medal winner from England Steven Scott celebrates his victory at the Barry Buddon Shooting centre Carnoustie

Image 98:
Australian Michael Shelley wins the Marathon

Image 99:
Adam Vella of Australia takes part in the Trap Men Shooting Qualification

Image 100:
Scotland's Samantha Kinghorn in the 1500m Para Sport Wheelchair – Women

Image 101:
Daniel Wallace
competes in the Men's
200m Individual Medley
Final at the Tollcross
International Swimming
Centre

Image 102:
Scotland's Daniel
Keatings win's silver in
the artistic gymnastics
men's individual
competition

Glasgow's Commonwealth Games: behind the scenes

Image 103:
England's Tiffany Porter competes in the women's 100m Hurdles final

Image 104:
Scotlands Ross Houston in the Men's Marathon

Image 105:
A competitor in the pole vault at Hampden

Image 106:
Team South Africa celebrate their involvement

"The approach taken in Glasgow to legacy has been different. The aim has been to ensure that legacies were planned, measurable and achieved alongside the Games"

Chapter 5
Building legacies

As we have seen in the previous chapters, from the outset the City Council and the Scottish Government had signalled their desire to ensure that hosting the Commonwealth Games in 2014 would generate a lasting legacy. This was made explicit in the bid for the 2014 Games, and reflected in particular the way that the City Council viewed the Games as an opportunity to help continue a process of transformation in the city. With continuing challenges in employment, health and wellbeing, and including more of the city's residents actively in the city's future, those involved with the Games wanted to ensure that benefits would be visible and measurable.

However, the experience of previous host cities of the Commonwealth Games and other major sporting events has suggested that generating lasting and meaningful legacies from such events is difficult. Almost all recent host cities of events such as the Commonwealth Games, Olympics or World Cups in football and rugby have indicated that they were seeking to use the event as a means to provide longer term benefits and impacts on communities. Despite such rhetoric, achieving benefits beyond that of new infrastructure has been hard to achieve. Even in the case of the London 2012 Olympics when the desire for legacy was outlined in advance of the events, delivering this has been difficult. And indeed legacy has often been pushed back, only becoming the focus of attention after the Olympics were over.

Learning from these experiences, and from other Commonwealth Games, the approach taken in Glasgow to legacy has been different. Here the aim has been to ensure that legacies were planned, visible, measurable and achieved *alongside* the delivery of the Games, rather than left to later or to chance. And many of these were planned to be delivered before the Games!

Planning legacy

Early in 2009 the City Council published its 'legacy framework' signalling not only the ways in which legacy would be achieved but also the guiding principles that would be applied to the planning of such legacies. It was constructed around three basic elements – a set of 6 themes which captured the main benefits which the council felt could be achieved by being host city, the creation of smaller projects which were nested under one (or in a few cases two) theme, and an assessment of the outcomes of each project over a 10 year period.

Importantly activity and investment made in the preparation for the Games and other resources available within the Council and its partners were planned to be used to help deliver legacy. Thus, for example, building new venues had to deliver legacy outcomes in terms of community use, greater levels of physical activity or club growth as well as providing a location for sport during the Games. And investment in improving the quality of the open space around venues for the Games was viewed as opportunities to involve local communities in creating them, and then providing attractive areas likely to increase levels of walking.

This approach sought to address the failure of many previous Games and major sporting events to derive long term benefits by ensuring legacies were created quickly and visibly before as well as after the event, and that actions planned for the Games should be focused on the long-term benefits as well as the needs of the event.

For the City Council, 6 themes formed the legacy framework – focusing on economic prosperity, a more active citizenry, a greener, accessible and inclusive city, and one that was internationally connected. Underpinning these were also 3 principles – healthy, sustainable and inclusive – and together the framework set out not only the longterm vision of creating a more active, healthy population but also a city which welcomes and integrates diversity as part of an economically and environmentally sustainable place.

Legacy themes

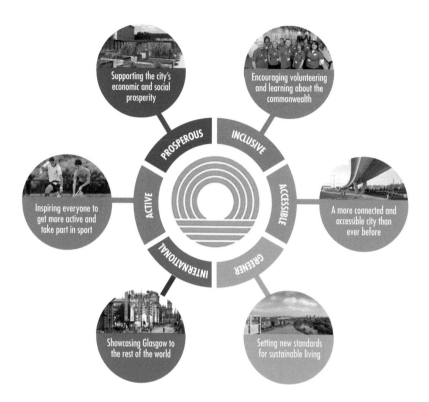

Associated with the 6 legacy themes, there have been 90 projects supported by the City Council, each helping to delivery tangible legacies in the city as a whole and in local communities. Many of these applied for the right to be awarded the city's legacy brand and over 300 projects have been recognised as contributing towards the legacy goals. The 100th project – St Paul's Youth Forum – was granted such status in February 2014 and typified the ways in which local community groups embraced the themes of the Games to help achieve impact locally.

Did you know?
Run by local groups, St Paul's Youth Forum, Blackhill,
supports young people through youth work including
after school programmes, parent and toddler groups
and indoor and outdoor activities. It runs its own local
youth radio station and, ahead of the Games, the young
people involved connected with partners in Zambia to
unite communities through a sharing of their different
experience of the Games.

Legacy projects – some examples

PROSPEROUS	ACTIVE	INTERNATIONAL	GREENER	ACCESSIBLE	INCLUSIVE
Business Portal	Active Health	Glasgow Destination Portal	Clean Glasgow	Dalmarnock Station Upgrade	Host City Volunteers/ Active Citizenship
Clyde Gateway URC	Playground to Podium	Strategic Major Events Forum	Low Emission Zones	Sustainable Transport Initiatives	Healthy World/Park Twinning
Commonwealth Apprenticeship Initiative	Scotstoun Leisure Centre	Glasgow Tourist Service Initiative	European Green Capital Award	Waking & Cycling network	Malawi Young Leaders of Learning
Community Benefit Policy	Cycling Strategy	2014 Cultural Plan	Commonwealth Gardens	Public Realm/ Velocity	

Delivering legacy

To help focus attention on legacy and to ensure that these ambitions
were being realised, new governance structures and processes have
been put in place by the Council.

Crucial to ensure that planning and delivering legacy were at the
heart of the preparation for the Games, one senior political leader
– Councillor Archie Graham – had responsibility for overall coordination of legacy. As depute Leader of the Council and executive
member for Culture and Sport, he was well positioned to ensure that
legacy from the Games was integrated into the normal business of the
Council and that existing service delivery and monitoring was also
utilised. Further, as the elected representative on the Glasgow 2014
Board and executive member for the Commonwealth Games, he has

been a champion at ensuring that legacy is at the forefront of Games delivery. He chaired the Glasgow 2014 Group, bringing together the key staff involved in each theme area.

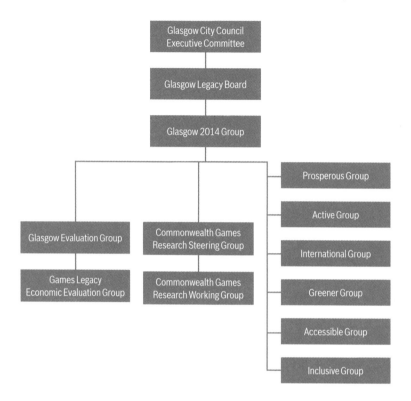

For each theme a working group, involving partners from across the city, was set up, each with the aim to define and help stimulate projects to achieve the overall legacy objectives. These groups were chaired by senior representatives from the Council family – termed Legacy Theme Champions – and a number of members of each working group were also involved in other groups to provide links between them. The work of these groups was supported by a small, dedicated team – the Council 2014 Team – who coordinated the production of regular progress reports.

Overseeing the development of legacy was a Legacy Board. Drawing its membership from outside of the Council, the Board had key leaders across the thematic areas – including the chief medical officer for Scotland, the former leader of regeneration associated with the Manchester 2002 Games, and Scottish athlete Lee McConnell.

LEGACY BOARD MEMBERSHIP

Cllr Gordon Matheson (Chair)
Leader of Glasgow City Council
Cllr Archie Graham
Depute Leader, Executive Member for the Commonwealth Games
Cllr Graeme Hendry
Leader of the Opposition, Glasgow City Council
Sir Harry Burns
Chief Medical Officer for Scotland
David Grevemberg
Chief Executive, Glasgow 2014 Organising Committee
Andrew Dearie
Young Person's Interaction Ambassador
Vicky Rosin
Assistant Chief Executive, Manchester City Council
Benny Higgins
Chief Executive Officer, Tesco Bank
Lee McConnell
Olympian and Commonwealth Athlete
Diane McLafferty
Scottish Government

Demonstrating that the intended legacies are being delivered is an important part of the process of creating benefits, and in Glasgow this task was led by the Glasgow Evaluation Group (GEG), chaired by the Executive Director of Development & Regeneration Services Richard Brown. Bringing together all the data and information on legacy projects, GEG developed its legacy evaluation framework providing a set of outcomes and key research questions which the legacy working groups were looking to achieve.

This organised approach to legacy and its evaluation is novel in the context of major sporting events, using techniques more commonly applied in other policy areas. As well as offering the City Council the advantage of bringing legacy into a single framework for reporting purposes, it has ensured that legacy outcomes form part of the discussions over each of the delivery processes of the Games. As a result, in advance of the Games some elements of legacy had already been secured.

And importantly – as acknowledged by the CGF in its assessment of Games planning in Glasgow – it has allowed many legacy projects to be integrated into the preparation for the Games. In this respect, legacy and event planning have come together.

Pre-games legacies

What are these pre-games legacies? The most obvious legacies are those which relate to the physical infrastructure constructed to help support the event. In Glasgow, these include the venues, the road infrastructure in the East End of the city and the extension of the M74 in the South of the city. However, as indicated in the bid, many of these projects were already being developed or planned and would have occurred without the Games coming to the city. However, the Games did help to bring forward delivery and they formed vital parts of the delivery of the event.

Other projects and initiatives are less obvious and visible but form important parts of the legacies generated by the Games. Some of these have already been mentioned in earlier chapters on the preparation of the bid, reflecting the intention that legacies created by and for the Games should become part of the mainstream activity of the city, and contribute towards the needs of citizens. The focus here is on a few examples of projects and activities which illustrate both the range of legacy under the 6 themes and the ways in which progress on legacy has been generated in advance of the event happening in 2014, and the integration into Games planning.

Under the prosperous theme, initiatives have primarily focused on ensuring that employment opportunities are available for Glasgow residents and businesses. The Glasgow Business Portal, Community Benefit Clauses, and the apprenticeship and employment funding and support (Chapter 4) formed two key dimensions – improving business growth and performance, and increasing employment and training opportunities. The third strand related to the physical appearance of the city, and focused on projects which upgraded public spaces, such as the waterfront upgrades and the regeneration programme of the East End (Chapter 4). The International theme has included projects focused on enhancing Glasgow's image (see Chapter 6) and the use of the sporting and cultural assets to attract leisure and business tourism. The Games has provided a focal point in the city's wider strategy in this area and at Games time included a Glasgow Business embassy to be hosted to promote the city's opportunities to delegations from across the world.

Whilst the improved sports infrastructure used during the Games was a key strand underpinning the active legacy theme, this ambitiously looked to inspire people to become more active and increase participation in sport. In previous Games and other sporting events the evidence of a sustained increase in the number of people involved in sporting activity and clubs has been lacking. Indeed, one of the trends has been for the Games facilities to help stimulate a short-term but unsustained increased use in the immediate aftermath of the Games.

Recognising that one challenge – faced in Britain after the London 2012 Olympics – was the lack of capacity within existing clubs and sports organisations to meet the post-event demand, a key part of the Glasgow legacy strategy has been supporting projects which seek to support clubs, coaches and volunteers. This looked beyond the investment in the physical sporting infrastructure to support the growth of club-based capacity. Collaboration with national sporting governing bodies and with SportScotland's legacy programme on club development (including its Clubmark scheme) is helping to augment more local initiatives backed by Glasgow Life. Investment has been made prior to the Games in coaching education and club development programmes.

This national scheme is designed to help clubs develop, providing not only a recognition of progress and planning by clubs, but an accreditation that can inspire confidence that the clubs are offering high quality standards and have aspirations for improvement. In Glasgow, more than 110 clubs across different sports have been helped to gain accreditation awards and many have experienced growth since they achieved this status.

Glasgow Life legacy programmes have provided support to local voluntary clubs to improve quality, grow membership, recruit volunteers and train coaches to a high standard. Since 2009 the number of clubs across all sports who engage with Glasgow Life initiatives has doubled to 636 by 2014, and there has been a growth in volunteers, coaches and club members over this period.

Did you know?
Since 2009, clubs assisted by Glasgow Life have already seen a benefit from the Games inspiring people to get involved. Membership has tripled to more than 16,500, the number of coaches has almost doubled to 3,800 and there has been a similar increase in volunteer helpers in clubs to more than 3,900 by 2014.

Under the active programme, there have been development pathway into sport, through club showcase events and taster sessions in Glasgow schools. In the last 5 years, more than 3,700 school-to-club links have been created.

To date, the evidence suggests that this twin approach to generating capacity within clubs and providing modern facilities has attracted many more people to be actively involved with organised clubs. However, there are also signs that across the city less formally organised forms of physical activity and sport are thriving too. The growth in the number of parkruns in Glasgow highlights this trend. Since starting in Pollok Park in 2008, the event has expanded and been supported under the Commonwealth Games legacy programme to include new venues in the east (Tollcross Park), north (Springburn Park) and west (Victoria Park) of the city.

Did you know?
Parkruns are weekly, timed 5k runs organised by volunteers and held in parks across the UK. Each week more than 50,000 people take part and more than 5,000 help organise. They are free to enter and anyone is encouraged to come along as and when they can.

The accessible Glasgow theme not only sought to improve the connectivity of the city through major transport infrastructure projects, but also to encourage active travel, moving away from cars to public transport, and to walking and cycling. Like many major cities, commuting to work is predominantly by car (41%) and, although the volume of cars in the city has declined slightly in recent years, Glasgow has the largest traffic volume in Scotland. Only a small proportion – about 2% – cycle to work each day, although this is a lower proportion than other major Scottish cities.

Since 2009, more than £10m has been invested within Glasgow in creating and upgrading the city's network of cycle paths and walkways. Much of this has been connected with the Games, enabling spectators to have the option of walking (or cycling) between venues and the city centre. New footbridges across the Clyde have helped to make connections over the river, and segregated cycle lanes have added to the safety of users in new routes from Hampden Park and Cathkin Braes and from the Emirates Arena.

The City Council has assisted this growth through the creation of a city Mass Cycle Hire scheme, with 400 bikes available in 2014 across 31 locations and set to double in 2015. Users can register as a member or as a casual user through a website, their Smartphone or by telephone and, with charges from £1 for 30 minutes, the scheme has appealed to corporate and university partners who have subscribed. During the Games, there were approximately 10,000 hires of the bikes. Glasgow Bike Station, the charity advocating mental and physical health through cycling as a means of transport won the contract to carry out all bike maintenance.

Sporting success in cycling both on the track and on the road has helped to increase the appeal of cycling. The Sir Chris Hoy Velodrome as the home of Scottish Cycling has provided an introduction to cycling for many families and school pupils with coach-led sessions experiencing high demand. Cycling clubs across the city too have experienced growth and in turn this has helped to increase commercial cycling centres and retailers.

This investment in active travel, as well as a commitment to a low carbon Games, forms part of Glasgow City Council's longer term aim of being one of Europe's most sustainable cities. A key part of the Greener legacy has been demonstrating through the Games possible ways in which communities can be involved in making the city more sustainable in the future. The approach builds on the Clean Glasgow campaign, developed several years in advance of the Games, to encourage residents and visitors to keep the city's public spaces safe and clean.

Across the city, local schools have been learning about the environment, food and biodiversity of the Commonwealth countries within a specific region. The selection of region was based on the Commonwealth Park twinning initiative which saw each school being twinned with a Commonwealth region and their local park in Glasgow. Children in every school in Glasgow were invited to design a picture and signs which connected their local hub park with the Commonwealth nations to which it is twinned – Europe (Bellahouston Park), Africa (Tollcross, Provan Hall and Pollok), Americas (Glasgow Green), Asia (Springburn and Queen's Park), Oceania (Botanic Gardens) and the Caribbean (Linn and Victoria Parks).

The award winning Stalled Spaces scheme has seen 84 projects bring 24 hectares of land which have adopted for community use. Each of these projects has transformed a vacant or under-utilised piece of land into temporary use, frequently for community use. The aim of the scheme is to allow communities to put forward imaginative ideas for support from the Council and through volunteering efforts bring communities together. All of the spaces are short-lived with the intention that more permanent facilities will get erected on the space over time. Winning awards for the participation by communities and city design, the Stalled Spaces scheme has attracted interest from across the city and involved, by 2014, more than 280 volunteers.

The remaining legacy theme – an inclusive Glasgow – was perhaps most specifically connected with the opportunities arising from being host city and the needs of the Games. The inclusive legacy theme set out to "encourage people in Glasgow to participate in volunteering programmes".

Volunteers are an important part of the success of mega-sporting events such as the Commonwealth Games. Over the years the numbers of Games volunteers has increased from 12,000 at Manchester in 2002, to 15,000 in Melbourne and 22,000 volunteers in Delhi in 2010 – named Delhi United – who worked alongside the 4,000 paid staff of the Organising Committee.

Glasgow – drawing on the experience of the handover in Delhi in 2010 and the London 2012 Olympics – sought volunteers for different roles.

Glasgow's Commonwealth Games: behind the scenes

Image 110:
Council workers clearing
up at Cathkin Braes

Image 111:
Mountain biking,
Cathkin Braes

Glasgow's Commonwealth Games: behind the scenes

Image 112:
The Legacy of the
Games – to be more
active, Science Centre

Image 113:
Volunteer driver waving
to the Crowds

Glasgow's Commonwealth Games: behind the scenes

About 12,500 were recruited by the OC as volunteers for the Games (the Clydesiders), and Glasgow Life recruited approximately 1,100 volunteers to help direct people across the city as Host City Volunteers.

The increasing public awareness of the role of volunteering at the Games has greatly assisted in the recruitment process. As was widely reported, the overwhelming response to the call for applications to be a Clydesider – around 51,000 applications – underlined the enthusiasm with which people from Glasgow, across Scotland and well beyond wanted to be part of the event. Recruiting the 12,500 people required became more challenging for the OC which had to increase the time and resources required to assess applications, conduct interviews and ascribe roles to selected volunteers. In addition, 3,000 volunteers were recruited to be part of the 'cast' performing at the Opening and Closing Ceremonies, and hundreds of Queen's Baton Relay batonbearers helped to take the baton across Scotland.

Did you know?
Proposals for the name of Clydesider volunteers originally included 'The Clan' and 'Games Stars'?

Within Glasgow there was a strong desire that opportunities to be volunteers would reach across all communities, including those from ethnic minorities, people with disabilities, and people from low income areas including those who had limited or no access to the internet – a requirement as applications to be a Clydesider had to be completed online. In an attempt to increase applications from these groups within Glasgow, the Council family were involved in helping to raise awareness of the Clydesider volunteering opportunities using advertising and information within its community facilities. Active steps were taken to help and give advice to potential applicants on how to complete the online forms. And support was made available in local community centres and libraries to help complete applications.

Did you know?
With funding from the Big Lottery Scotland and from
the Spirit of 2012 Trust, more than £550,000 was
provided to help volunteers as Clydesiders or members
of the cast who struggled to fulfil their commitments
because of low income, carer responsibilities or
disabilities. This fund, called the Volunteer Support Pot,
helped 2,177 individuals and 7 groups.

For those offered positions as Clydesiders, a scheme - the Volunteer Support Pot - was funded by the Big Lottery Fund. This provided financial assistance towards some of the cost of attending training and fulfilling their volunteer roles and was targeted at those on low incomes or struggling to pay for travel and subsistence. The support was initially available for Clydesiders from across Scotland but was later extended to the rest of the UK. All of which was aimed at boosting the number of applications and volunteers from communities and groups who were often under-represented in the volunteer 'army' in the past.

Whilst supportive of the desire to make volunteering opportunities as inclusive as possible, the OC had a legal requirement to avoid discrimination in the selection process. Given the finite budget and resources available, their imperative was to recruit suitably able and qualified volunteers into the necessary roles as efficiently as possible. With the enormous public interest to be a Clydesider, there was already significant pressure on the volunteer team in the OC in processing applications, arranging and conducting interviews, and responding to information requests from applicants.

Greater opportunity to recruit from these groups under represented within the Host City Volunteer Programme which saw 1,100 volunteers being ambassadors for the city at key areas across the city centre and between venues to help people find their way, and provide information about Glasgow. A different and ambitious approach was used by Glasgow Life for the recruitment of these Host City Volunteers (HCVs). With funding from the City Council and the Big Lottery Fund, and with the assistance of community groups working with people with disabilities, in some of the more deprived parts of the city, and with other minorities, the HCV programme was more than just a Games volunteering opportunity. Specific training was provided about the city and the events, teams were formed to help support each of the volunteers and team leaders were appointed to help each volunteer gain benefits. The aim of the programme was not only to help at the Games but to assist each person in terms of their confidence, their ability to engage with the public and encourage them to have roles as volunteers in their communities.

Did you know?
An exhibition called "Our Games" showcasing the experiences of Host City Volunteers was held in the People's Palace, Glasgow, in 2015. The exhibition was co-produced with the HCVs working with Glasgow Museum staff.

The enormous enthusiasm and support provided by the volunteers - as Clydesiders, Host City Volunteers, as members of the cast during the Games and in making the Queen's Baton Relay special for each community it visited - was widely acknowledged as an important part of the success of the Glasgow Commonwealth Games. They were, for many thousands of people, the 'face of the Games' - a key part of the festival effect of the Games.

Harnessing that enthusiasm and translating it into a legacy for the city and local communities forms part of Glasgow's Strategic Volunteering Framework and schemes such as the Host City Volunteers will continue as volunteers are offered opportunities to be more involved with sports and community organisations and through the continuing Glasgow Citizenship programme.

Taking forward success

In seeking to redefine the timeframes used to plan and assess legacy, the Glasgow approach has been an important test for future events. Demonstrating that legacies can be produced in advance of the event itself as well as generated through the success of hosting the Games has been at the heart of the city's planning for legacy.

As with all major investments, time will be required to allow a more complete judgement of the impact and effect the Games had on the city. Studies based on previous events suggest that impacts are often limited to the infrastructure left behind after the event and that no previous host nation has demonstrated a sustainable positive health impact as a result of a major sporting event.

And there are of course risks that with the spotlight turned off from the Games, with existing projects ending and with public funding for legacy initiatives having to compete with other emerging priorities, the momentum already existing will be lost.

Importantly there is a recognition in the City Council that in creating a Games legacy, the analogy is of a 'marathon rather than a sprint'. To achieve its aims, the values and enthusiasm of the Commonwealth Games will have to become an embedded part of the lives of Glaswegians. The final test will be whether volunteers are still inspired to get involved, whether the opportunities for more active travel are being taken, more people are using facilities for physical activity and there is greater community involvement in improving their lives and well-being.

The Glasgow experience suggests that the prognosis for achieving a meaningful and lasting legacy is good. For the next 5 years, Glasgow City Council and the Scottish Government will both be continuing to monitor the legacies for the Games with expectations that, by 2019, the city will still be able to demonstrate that it did as much as possible to ensure that there were lasting legacies. Importantly too, the CGF in their pre-Games assessment of the readiness of Glasgow for the Games were quick to acknowledge the novelty of this approach – and to endorse it. In their view, the legacy planning and structures for the Games developed by the City Council and partners was likely to be the blueprint for all future Commonwealth Games. And for the city and its residents, there are already tangible legacies which have involved many more people than with any previous Games.

"Changing the marketing approach in the lead up to the Games was a bold and imaginative step"

Chapter 6
Sharing the vision; communicating the message

Walking (or cycling) around the city during the Games, it was difficult to miss a central message being portrayed about the city - People
Make Glasgow. From the vast display on the front of the City College
building overlooking the city centre and visible from the mountain
bike trails at Cathkin Braes on the southern outskirts of the city, to the
banners on bridges and map-posts, and on the much sought after pin
badges being handed out at locations across the city, the new brand
took pride of place.

Indeed, People Make Glasgow became one of the defining images of
the Games representing the next stage in the city's transformation
from the Miles Better brand in the 1990s and the later Glasgow: Scotland with Style brand, both of which sought to change perceptions of
the city.

    Changing the city marketing approach in the lead up to the Games
was a bold and imaginative step, being the first times that a host city
had taken the decision to make such a significant 'freshening up' of
its marketing slogan ahead of the sporting event. Although renowned
for being a welcoming city, the new People Make Glasgow brand gave
recognition to Glasgow's citizens being at the heart of its future.

    This message also had an important part to play in relation to Glas-
gow's vision of the Commonwealth Games. Within the city, it sought
to include all communities, saying to Glaswegians that this was their
Games, and they could he proud of the event. And beyond the city, the
People Make Glasgow brand acknowledged the contribution of visitors and spectators from across the world.

    Throughout the planning of the Commonwealth Games in Glas-
gow, from the bid onwards, there has been a consistent vision that the
Games in Glasgow would support change in the city. The vision had
three parts:

- A Games that celebrated the connection between sport and culture

- A Games helping to change Glasgow

- A Games in Glasgow showing the continuing relevance of the Commonwealth Games and their values of humanity, dignity and equality.

On the journey in preparing for 2014, the partners have sought to reinforce these messages – at Delhi in 2010, by linking community activity with the Games across the city, at the Games ceremonies and in the way that Glasgow was presented around the world through the event.

Delhi Handover: "a warm invitation from the city of Glasgow"
The first opportunity to signal to an international audience the essence of Glasgow's ambitions for the Games came at the formal handover of the Commonwealth flag at the end of the previous Games.

Although there is a degree of formality about the process of 'handover', the closing ceremony of the Commonwealth Games has in recent decades become more of a party: an opportunity for the current host city to reflect on the success of the event and 'let their hair down' as athletes and spectators revel in their own endeavours and those of the city. And for the next host city, the closing ceremony is also a chance to set out its intentions to welcome the Commonwealth in four years' time.

For the closing ceremony in Delhi in 2010, the Glasgow 2014 OC agreed that the City Council would take the lead role in commissioning the celebrations. In an innovation which reflected the values of community and volunteering, 348 dancers were brought together as a cast to mark out the Glasgow and Scottish theme in the 8 minutes slot of the closing ceremony in Delhi. The cast included representatives from each local authority across Scotland and, reflecting the desire for the 2014 Games to be inclusive, the cast participants were diverse, including people with disabilities.

As they followed onto the stage the lone piper, the cast sent out a message of "a warm invitation from the city of Glasgow to the nations, athletes and peoples of the Commonwealth to come and join us in 2014".

The organisation of the handover was different to that of most previous Games, with a deliberate strategy of a local team from Glasgow Life leading the planning of the event, rather than the usual contracting of the ceremony to external experts. As a result the city gained benefits from the £1.8m spent on the ceremony. This approach was designed to allow the knowledge and skills learnt from organising the handover to be retained by staff working in the city. These lessons have been used by the Glasgow team in organising other events in the city, and helped in the development of the festival elements of the Games in 2014. There were other valuable lessons too. Despite the logistical challenges of transporting 350 people to India and the lack of prior experience of many of the cast in performing in public, the success of the Delhi Flag Handover showed the potential value of increasing the confidence and social skills of individuals with no prior experience of participation. For some of those in Delhi, they continued to be ambassadors for, and volunteered at, the Games.

Positive reports in the UK press the next day and the claim from the Times of India newspaper that the performances from the Glasgow cast 'stole the show', eclipsing other aspects of the Delhi Closing Ceremony, enhanced the confidence of the Glasgow partners that they could deliver an event that was inclusive and accessible.

Connecting Glaswegians to the Games

The Delhi Flag Handover helped to provide connections with other Commonwealth nations, but within Glasgow, achieving such a unified sense of celebration and welcome had not been as easy a task. As the city started its preparation for the Games in 2007 and 2008, there was understandable friction within communities in parts of the city distant from the building of venues and related projects. With Games activity focused on three clusters - in the east around the Emirates Arena and Celtic Park, in the west around the SECC and Scotstoun, and in the south at Hampden and Ibrox - residents in other areas struggled to feel connected with the Games. This is in part an almost inevitable outcome of the desire by the CGF for Games facilities and venues to be co-located, enabling easy access for athletes and spectators at the Games. However for the host city, such a concentration inevitably means that other parts of the city were less visibly connected with the Games.

Mindful of this, the Council and agencies made a conscious and planned attempt to encourage people across the city to get involved and for communities to feel part of the developing celebration. The Council developed a 'Guide to Getting Involved' indicating the many ways in which communities could be part of the celebration. As well as offering information on its dedicated webpage, consultation meetings and workshops were held across the city with local community groups to provide help and inspiration to residents to feel part of the Games. In addition, events were held across local communities in local centres under the 'Inspiring Communities' banner to get involved, attended by more than 500 people. Both of these approaches also provided important opportunities for the Council to lay out its ambitions and visions for legacy, and to showcase some of the Council-led projects which were being supported.

Most of these projects took time to be created but gradually initiatives were set up to include communities across the city – some through schools and learning centres where the focus was on connecting the Commonwealth with the curriculum, others more connected with their daily lives and the city's legacy themes. Initially there was a tendency to badge existing schemes as part of the demonstration of a Commonwealth Games 'legacy' but, as the time of the Games got nearer, more communities become aware of the values of the Games and were able to generate new and imaginative projects.

Community based legacy projects

One of the most successful ways in which communities were encouraged to feel connected with the Games was by them being branded as a Games legacy project. With approval from the CGF and the OC, a special Commonwealth Games Legacy brand was developed for the city, with the logo of 'A Games Legacy for Glasgow'. Projects, activities and events which met the ambition of at least one of the six legacy themes and which contributed to sustainability, health and inclusion were able to apply for use of the logo. Importantly these activities did not need to be at all Games related. Instead the emphasis was on how local people or groups were helping in their own way and area to deliver the city-wide aims – reinforcing the longer term planning of connecting the Games with the lives of local people.

In total 316 projects across the city were granted the Games Legacy for Glasgow logo. Projects were hugely varied, with some being small, one-off celebratory events, but others involved thousands of people in city-wide initiatives. The Scottish Tourist Guide Association, for example, received recognition for its 'Commonwealth Games tour' project, providing training and support for guides who lead tours around the venues and sites of the city. And the North West Women's Centre based in Maryhill in the north west of the city took the initiative to design a 'Commonwealth garden'. Supporting its work in providing a range of social and educational opportunities for local women, the gardens provided a backdrop to teach children about the countries of the Commonwealth - and provide a lasting resource for the community group.

Each of the projects however had to illustrate their connections with the city's legacy themes. Play on Pedals - a project to enable pre-school children across the city to learn how to ride bikes was supported to expand its role in connecting cycling and play. More than 7,500 four-year olds have now been taught and the project continues to grow, having received new bikes and storage facilities in the city. The cycling theme also features in the Glasgow-Lahore Cycle Challenge, set up by a team of cyclists to raise money for the Yorkhill Children's Charity in Glasgow and the Children's Hospital/Institute in Lahore through their endeavours and by reinforcing the Games legacy theme of health and physical activity.

Did you know?
In 2013-14, 202 of the community-led Glasgow legacy projects shared £12.7m from the City Council's Integrated Grant Fund, available to deliver much needed services to citizens.

Different service areas also contributed towards building legacies, showing how routine activities could be developed into legacy benefits for local people. The development of play-areas, for example, within the Glasgow Housing Association (GHA) managed sites became spaces supporting increases in sports and physical activity, whilst with support from Education Services all the schools in the city engaged in local activities and learning which made direct connections with the Commonwealth and the Games.

Image 115:
The crowds gather in
Glasgow city centre and
in the Merchant City

Glasgow's Commonwealth Games: behind the scenes

Building stronger connections

Whilst such badging of projects as legacy helped to engage communities, a more sophisticated approach emerged over time from the Council and city partners that generated more tangible and understandable links with the Games, and beyond, with the legacy themes (Chapter 5). This process of learning occurred both within the Council's senior managers and with local delivery teams as they became more confident about how to build local community links, and found ways to draw in other partners across Scotland.

One example of this was in the arena of education. For schools, the emergence of Game On Scotland – and its local variation Game On Glasgow – offered an education programme related to Glasgow 2014 and events in Scotland. The teaching resources linked to curricula areas from health and wellbeing to sciences and technologies. In Glasgow other projects with school pupils focused on how they could be involved in making their own links with the Games, and the opportunities which they offered. With active involvement from the OC and the City Council, pupils were encouraged to participate in various competitions – as diverse as the designs of the Clyde Mascot and the 25 Clyde sculptures in the Clyde Trail, through to the art which was displayed in the Athletes' Village during the Games.

Did you know?
Game On Glasgow was part of a national programme
which provided support to teachers, school leaders
and education managers in creating stimulating
learning experiences for young people from 3-18 using
the Commonwealth Games as a context for learning.
Designed to help support the Curriculum for Excellence
it was a partnership with Education Scotland, the
Scottish Government, the OC and Glasgow City Council.

As the Games approached, it became easier to make more direct links. The Glasgow School's Baton Relay provided an inclusive project to allow schools to be connected with the Queen's Baton Relay as it progressed across the world during 2013 and 2014. Organised by the Council's Active Schools coordinators, more than 70 schools and nurseries took part in this relay across the city. Mirroring the Queen's Baton Relay as it crossed the 71 nations and territories of the Commonwealth, the specially designed Baton was transported to schools twinned with the relevant countries of the Commonwealth. Each school was encouraged to offer imaginative ways to transport the baton and to use the visit of the baton to focus more on the other Commonwealth country and their own links with sport and physical activity.

Did you know?
The Glasgow Schools baton was designed by Liam Doherty from St Andrew's Secondary school which was made specially by local company Product Design. It was carried for more than 200 miles as it weaved its way across the city.

The underlying message of sport and wellbeing was a central element of the Gold Medal Programme. This project sought to inspire young people in schools across the city to try a new sport or get involved in cultural activities. Funding of £55,000 was provided by Glasgow Housing Association (GHA) and Cube Housing Association to support applications from schools and to bring the best of these together in a 'showcase' event in the Emirates Arena in March 2014 ahead of the Games. A wide range of imaginative projects were supported, each helping to connect sport with healthy living and reinforce the connections between sport and culture.

The connections between the Commonwealth and communities were used as the basis for the Glasgow Hub Park Twinning project. Local parks at the heart of communities became the focal point for links with Commonwealth Regions. One of the most obvious symbols was the erection of a giant wooden sculpture of the official Glasgow 2014 Commonwealth Games mascot, Clyde, in Queen's Park to the south of the city centre. The 2.4 metre (eight feet) tall creation was skilfully carved by local sculptor Robert Coia with the help of primary six pupils from St Bride's Primary School who helped produce the stepping stones that surround the statue. It formed one of 12 intricately hand-carved sculptures placed within parks across the city as part of Glasgow City Council's Commonwealth Hub Parks Twinning Initiative. The parks were used as educational hubs where pupils learnt about sustainability, nature and the environment. Schools visited their partner park and participated in a variety of practical, active and outdoor learning experiences. Over the 4 years up to the Games, more than 12,000 pupils attended sessions run by Countryside Rangers to talk about crops from around the world, nature conservation, environmental impact and sustainability.

Image 116:
Relaxing on
George Square

Image 117:
Host City Volunteer
at Glasgow Green

Opinion surveys across the city since 2007 have consistently shown very high levels of support for the Games themselves and for the decision to host them in Glasgow. More than 85% of respondents have been in favour of the event, but far fewer initially felt that the benefits of the Games would touch them. As the summer of 2014 approached, and the events across the city increased, there was a rise in the number of Glaswegians being 'touched' by the Games.

Joining in with the Games

Developing a shared vision that has brought the city and its citizens and businesses together has required a coordinated and planned approach. Across the Council, each area of activity has found ways to help the development of new projects (or reinvigoration of existing projects) that more clearly were linked with a legacy goal. This has helped communities across the entire city to become more involved. And it has helped within the Council teams to get a clearer sense of how their activities – new and existing – are contributing to generating a lasting legacy.

As the city turned to focus on the Games in 2014, other types of projects have been generated to help increase visibility 'on the street'. Local businesses and communities were encouraged to display their support for the Games, although as required by the Commonwealth Games Act (2008) there was enforcement of the legal and limited use of official logos and brands. An imaginative solution was found by which businesses many of them small, independent commercial activities were able to access an online toolkit from the OC to download material to show their support for the Games and to use a specially developed brand.

One approach organised by a partnership between the City Council, Glasgow Life, Creative Scotland and Clyde Gateway sought to encourage communities, businesses and individuals to be linked together through the use of art in public places. The programme – named VeloCity– developed a small number of projects in areas of Glasgow which used art and the backdrop of the Commonwealth Games to help bring 'repair' or 'reconnect' communities.

Amongst the inspirations for VeloCity was the successful way public art was used around the London 2012 Olympics to help connect communities. Drawing on sporting themes but extending this to public artwork, various organisations had helped to build bridges within and between communities in the 6 London Boroughs around the Queen Elizabeth Olympic Park. VeloCity sought to develop this concept and apply it to Glasgow, both in connection with the Commonwealth Games and as part of a longer term project of using public art in development links within communities. The operational plan developed in 2012 envisaged clusters of activity associated with the venue areas in the east, south and west of the city, and with connections made between them through public art in corridors into the city centre.

Achieving this has been difficult, and many aspects of the scheme had to be scaled back due to limited funding and the difficult economic circumstances in which businesses and communities found themselves. In particular, opportunities to have art displayed across the city were more limited than expected. However, the principles were exemplified by the projects that have emerged, and they have helped to inspire others to use public art.

The Baltic Street playground project in the Dalmarnock area was an important development, bringing the community most affected by the new venue construction to see how some empty spaces could be brought to life and used for play and art. The team commissioned from Create London and Assemble worked with the local community to get them to view the area as a site for 'play'. And then, working with local youth workers, contractors and businesses as well as with the community, the site was landscaped to create a playground.

A Community Interest Company was set up to manage the site, and much of the work was delivered by local young people, many struggling in education or getting into employment.

Did you know?
The VeloCity project is continuing after the Games and there remains a commitment to find imaginative ways in which public art and its production can help bring communities together.

Initiatives such as this not only provided more attractive environments, but can be symbolically important locally too. Baltic Street had been at the industrial heart of the community in the past, including the location of the primary school and evokes strong memories amongst local residents of the area's rich past. The transformation of this space into a playground with the involvement of the local community has helped to make connections between the past and the future development of the area around sport and culture.

In contrast other art projects, such as the 2014 Sporting Mural project, were more directly related to the Games. Large murals on the side of buildings were commissioned by Glasgow 2014 to coincide with their ticketing campaign. Located in the Merchant City (depicting badminton) and at Partick transport interchange, the idea has been used by other organisations in advance of the Games. Murals were commissioned by the University of Strathclyde and City of Glasgow College for their buildings.

The Queen's Baton Relay (QBR)

However, undoubtedly one of the most potent symbols of the values of the Games and the strongest connection of communities with the Games is associated with the Queen's Baton Relay. Although originally only travelling between communities in the host nation, since 1958 the Baton has travelled the world to include every nation and territory invited to be present at the Games. It symbolises the host city and nation reaching out to welcome everyone to the Games, and in turn has become a symbol of unity across each country.

Organising the QBR route is a major logistical exercise, covering all 71 members of the Commonwealth. Even in the UK as the baton travelled from the Channel Islands to the north of Scotland, the organisation requires partnership between local police forces, local authorities and the Games partners. And with continuous media coverage of the event – either televised or through online streaming – there are competing desires to ensure local places are well represented.

Whilst the OC was responsible for the overall coordination, this was one aspect where the CGS were adamant that they retained responsibility for the QBR in Scotland. They oversaw the selection process of the 4000 batonbearers from the thousands of nominations received, with the judging panel selecting the successful bearers for each local authority. And with the OC, they planned the QBR route to visit 400 towns and villages over 40 days.

As host city, Glasgow was the final destination of the baton, reaching the city from its tour of Scotland on 20 July, 2014. The City Council and Glasgow Life recognised the importance of the QBR to help bring together communities across the city as part of the celebration.

As the Baton had progressed across the country, thousands of people had welcomed the bearers as they ran and walked through the local towns and villages. In Glasgow, special parties were held at the end of the three days when the Queen's Baton was in the city as well as a special 'start line' event at the start of each day's journey. Entry was free but by ticket to enable a fair distribution to those who wanted to attend. A ballot was held for each of the parties in Springburn Park in the north of the city, Victoria Park in the west and Queen's Park in the south.

Up to 8000 people attended each evening and were entertained not only by the batonbearers and musical events, but with the focus on bringing together culture and sport and, with a family atmosphere, the parks were transformed into 'come and try' sports alongside arts and dance activities. Hugely successful in terms of the festival atmosphere, the events also provided a fitting tribute to the batonbearers who had been selected primarily because of their connections with the local communities.

As with other Games events held outside of the main venues – the marathon and bike races – the route was selected to provide an opportunity to showcase Glasgow. A balance was struck between including as many communities in the city (the Baton was carried through each of the city's 21 wards) and iconic landmarks. From the start of each day at one of these – People's Palace in Glasgow Green, the Riverside Museum and the Tall Ship, and at Cathkin Braes – the baton passed through local high streets and shopping areas as well as cultural and sporting buildings. This enabled local communities to take their own initiative and provide street entertainment or other forms of welcome, which many did focused primarily on young people.

The batonbearers were selected not only as recognition for their contribution to sport or their local communities, but as ambassadors. Although most were already committed to volunteering, many of the QBR bearers have become more involved in their communities, helping to support clubs and organisations, or raising funds for good causes.

The Opening Ceremony

For any host city, the most important way to communicate their message comes with the two formal ceremonies of the Games, and especially the opening ceremony. Watched by an estimated one billion people across the world live and many more through recorded media it provides a unique opportunity to portray aspects of the city and country. And yet it is also one of the most challenging and potentially difficult elements of the Games.

Public expectations of the ceremony have grown enormously since the first Commonwealth Games were held in Hamilton in Canada. There the opening ceremony saw the traditional parade of athletes being watched by a few hundred spectators, many of whom were the officials. With enormous television exposure, the opening ceremonies of the Olympics, FIFA World Cup or the Commonwealth Games have become major spectacles in their own rights.

There are still of course some of the same traditional elements. The parade of athletes, the formal welcome from the Commonwealth Games Federation and the host nation; and the message delivered from the Queen as Head of the Commonwealth are essential. But there is now also an expectation of fireworks, music and dance, and a more dynamic show within the stadium.

Even though the Games are not nearly as large as the Olympics, public expectations are often of the same scale and Glasgow's opening ceremony inevitably attracted comparisons with that of the London 2012 Olympics. With a budget less than a tenth of that in London and a tiny fraction of that in Beijing in 2008, the Glasgow organisers had to think carefully about the ceremonies in order to meet both the formal and public expectations.

Responsibility for the ceremonies was shared between the host city - with Glasgow Life being the lead agency - and the OC, with a joint team coordinating planning. They commissioned Jack Morton Worldwide to deliver the ceremonies, an international organisation which has a strong track record in major sporting event ceremonies. In developing the brief given to Jack Morton about the vision and design of the opening ceremony, the Glasgow team were adamant that even with a tight budget, there was also a desire to redefine the nature of the opening ceremony. Their vision was that alongside traditional elements, three themes had to be central to the ceremony:

- an acknowledgement of the role that the Games were having in the process of change in Glasgow, looking beyond sport and culture to see how the city's communities were changing (this included local communities contributing to the countdown)

- a celebration of the values and ethos of the Commonwealth of equality and destiny, and how it continued to have relevance in the 21st century (shown by the UNICEF projects and the 'Glasgow Kiss')

- the importance of sport and culture coming together, not just in Glasgow but also as a means to inspire young people to make the most of their lives (through sportsmen and women illustrating the role of sport in changing lives across the Commonwealth)

The opening ceremony on the evening of 23 July, 2014 was watched by an estimated billion people worldwide, and it got people across the globe talking, creating thousands of messages, tweets and videos - most liking it, some being confused and some finding fault with it. It certainly created strange, perhaps unexpected outcomes - such as the boom in sales of the Tunnock's teacake. The vision of dancers dressed in Tunnock's teacakes and the procession of athletes led by Scottie dogs probably form some of the more abiding memories of the opening ceremony. The humble teacake, created by the family run business in Uddingston on the outskirts of the city was an unlikely symbol for the ceremony. It caught both the public imagination and the spirit of the event. And overall the opening ceremony was met with public enthusiasm and achieved exactly what was planned - 'a successful start' to the Games.

Image 118:
The Glasgow 2014
Commonwealth Games
Opening Ceremony
Rehearsal, Ibrox
Stadium

Image 119:
Film of John Barrowman
on Finnieston Crane
shown at Opening
Ceremony rehearsal

Glasgow's Commonwealth Games: behind the scenes

But the opening ceremony was more than just a spectacle, it helped to communicate the central ethos and values of the Games more explicitly and inclusively than in other Games of recent times. The inclusion of the partnership with UNICEF reinforced the values of humanity, dignity and equality, with the appeal at the Games not only raising over £5m but creating the connections between nations that is the central purpose of the Commonwealth and underlining the continued relevance of the Commonwealth to help alleviate poverty and make a difference in young people's lives. And the much acclaimed inclusion of the same-sex 'Glasgow Kiss' by entertainer John Barrowman underlined the support for gay rights.

The Red Road flats and the ceremony: an explosive mix

Arguably less powerfully portrayed was the Games' role in changing Glasgow. In planning for the ceremony, the intention had been a much more explicit and visible feature of urban change, represented by the inclusion of the live demolition of the Red Road flats.

The idea of including their demolition had originated at the very early stages of the planning of the ceremony. For those involved, the central vision was using the demolition of these symbolic parts of the Glasgow's landscape to link together Glasgow's story of urban regeneration and the Games. Much work was undertaken to capture and record for the ceremony the views of local residents, the role the flats had had in Glasgow history, and the connections with immigrants and asylum seekers from around the world welcomed to the city who had been the last residents in some of the tallest housing blocks in Europe. The plan had also been to talk about the next stage of the area and the plans for contemporary, sustainable housing.

The idea resonated with both the Glasgow Housing Association (GHA), owners of the flats, and the OC. The GHA were involved with a long-term and ambitious programme of renewal of the social housing stock across the city, including the replacement of many of the high rise tower blocks that had for nearly 50 years been a defining feature of the skyline of Glasgow. For the OC and the ceremonies team, the demolition provided an explosive dimension to the ceremony and symbolised the role of the Games in changing the city and the future of people's lives. As the video accompanying the announcement of the plan indicated, other leaders across the city also recognised the symbolism associated with the demolition and with the Red Road flats in particular as part of the city's community history.

As with all aspects of the opening ceremony, the details of the content was kept secret, discussed only by those directly involved and then with the proviso that they did not reveal details. The inclusion of such a public dimension to the ceremony, however, could not be kept secret until the Games. Local residents were inevitably going to be affected and preparations would have been public anyway. In the planning process a crucial point was reached when a public announcement had to be made so that consultations could be held with those involved.

This proposal for demolition had been discussed at the Scottish Government's Glasgow 2014 Strategic Group meeting on Tuesday 1 April, when the OC outlined the development of the concept of the live demolition being part of the opening ceremony. Represented by the senior staff, the OC reported on the consultations with other agencies and the detailed operational plan that was prepared. The group agreed to a public announcement on 3 April "to enable the community engagement exercise to commence".

This announcement was made by the media team at the OC on April 3rd:

> "Glasgow's iconic skyscraper symbols of the past – the Red Road tower blocks – will be demolished LIVE during the opening ceremony of the Commonwealth Games; a bold and dramatic statement of intent from a city focused on regeneration and a positive future for its people.
>
> The blow-down of five of the six remaining blocks, at one time the tallest residential structures in Europe, will take just 15 seconds and be the biggest demolition of its kind ever seen in Europe.
>
> This spectacular event will be beamed live into Celtic Park via the record-breaking 100 metre-wide screen occupying the entire south stand of the stadium, creating Glasgow's 'Window to the Commonwealth'.

It will form part of the opening ceremony, the curtain raiser to the largest sporting and cultural event Scotland has ever hosted."

As part of the announcement, a video was released which captured some of the sense of community which had formed around those involved in building the flats in the 1970s, and had contributions from GHA (David Fletcher, GHA Director of Regeneration, and Enrico Amato, GHA Environmental Co-ordinator), Gordon Matheson, Leader of Glasgow City Council and Dr Bridget McConnell, Chief Executive of Glasgow Life, as well as Patricia Ferguson, MSP (and former resident in Red Road).

The announcement created many more reactions than anticipated. For many of those involved in the discussions of the plans there was dismay that an explanation of the underlying context of this as part of the regeneration story was underplayed and then lost in the public reactions. For those who did not know about it, especially local residents, there was a huge element of surprise and a sense of exclusion. And for others, many of them outside of Glasgow, there was a rally call to oppose this being part of the opening ceremony 'celebrations'.

Whilst the video accompanying the press release from the OC recognised some of the sentiments and emotions attached to the flats as part of Glasgow's history, the press statements badly misrepresented the wider sentiment of the citizens of Glasgow. Within a few hours of the announcements the divisive nature of the decision was evident from public comments across a wide range of media. A formal petition was started in the next few days - eventually capturing more than 17,000 signatures. Most of this attention focused not on the symbolism of change for a better future, but on the historical and contemporary nature of the Red Road flats.

Despite efforts in the following days to explain the rationale for the inclusion of the live demolition in the ceremony and statements that the demolition plans would proceed, media and public attention by the end of the week was seeking a review of the decision. Over the first weekend, and under pressure, Police Scotland issued a statement indicating that with the heightened level of public concern and the risk of protests, they had significant concerns over safety around the demolition being part of the Games' ceremony.

The risk, deemed 'high', of keeping any potential protest and public intervention away from the demolition became too great. Drawing on the Police Scotland statement - reiterated in the Scottish Government convened Strategic Group that "public safety would always take precedence over the requirements of the ceremony" – on Sunday, April 7 the decision to remove this from the opening ceremony was announced.

Whilst the loss of this element of the ceremony plan was not crucial to its integrity, it did diminish the contribution of Glasgow's story of regeneration and renewal, which would have connected with the story being enacted through dance and music which formed a central message at the start of the ceremony.

More significantly, the Red Road flats debate underlined the importance of clear and well-explained communication of the purpose of the Games and its elements in order to gain public support. In putting forward the idea of the demolition as a large public announcement without careful explanation to journalists, the central points of the contribution the Red Road flats had made to the regeneration of the city were quickly lost.

Did you know?
The 5.5m high Big 'G' in George Square which formed the backdrop of thousands of photographs is to be retained and re-housed as a permanent display.

People Make Glasgow

In contrast to the Red Road flats issues, the decision to re-brand the city was a more inclusive affair and received enormous public accolades as well as positive press coverage. The decision to change the overall brand used by the Glasgow City Marketing Bureau to promote the city during the lead up to the Games was a brave – and some suggested at the time potentially foolhardy – decision. There was a recognition that the brand mattered. Since the success of the Glasgow's Miles Better campaign launched by Michael Kelly in 1983, there has been a wider acknowledgement that keeping the brand used for Glasgow contemporary was essential. However, to do this during the lead up to the Games was a challenge.

The necessity for this, however, was also clear. The award winning 'Glasgow: Scotland with Style' was 10 years old and needing some refreshment as the city and its competitors had moved on. Like its successful predecessor, the brand continued to have some resonance in supporting international tourism, retailing and the cultural sectors, but it was no longer reinforcing other key aspirations for the future. The Glasgow: Scotland with Style brand had limited connection with the emerging areas of bioscience, innovation, energy and higher education which formed key platforms of the new economic strategy.

In a bold departure from the established practice of using design consultants to propose designs and logos, GCMB and the Council decided in 2013 to ask people across the city, Scotland and internationally what should form the basis of a new brand for Glasgow. With more than 1500 opinions expressed through the website, and views of more than 40 of the key leaders of private, public and academic sectors of the city sought by Edinburgh-based Tayburn, the next challenge was distilling these into a single, coherent brand that aligned with the ambitions of the city agencies. The dilemma was to select between those aspects which celebrated the physical fabric of the city (especially its architecture and parks), its history and contribution to the world (through culture and innovation) or those about Glasgow being friendly and welcoming.

As Councillor Gordon Matheson, Leader of the Council, said in launching the new brand in May, the focus on people was overwhelmingly the preferred choice:

"Glasgow is a warm, welcoming and genuinely friendly city, because the people are. We're an ambitious, inventive and entrepreneurial city, because the people are. And we're a down to earth, to the point, no nonsense city, because the people are. We work well together, we get things done and we make things happen".

The People Make Glasgow brand was created by Glasgow-based Tangent Graphic to give expression to this formed a high profile and very visible dimension during the Commonwealth Games. And if the evidence from the messages left by departing visitors at Glasgow Airport on their 'memory tree' are representative of the thousands who came to the city, the brand admirably captured their over-riding sentiment – it was indeed the people of the city that helped make most visitors' memories.

During the Games the People Make Glasgow slogan reinforced the vision and message that had been a consistent part of the Glasgow Commonwealth Games story; one which celebrated the diversity of the city, welcoming people from across the Commonwealth – not just at Games time but through its recent history – and one where the changing physical landscape was one made for, and by, its people.

Glasgow's Commonwealth Games: behind the scenes

214

"Hundreds of thousands of people were thronging the streets, parks and sporting venues across the city, creating an atmosphere of celebration and festivity"

Chapter 7
'Bring it on': coordinating city planning

As the banners started to appear around the city in the weeks leading up to the start of the Games, there was both a sense of anticipation amongst citizens and an unusual calm. When the schools closed for the summer holidays at the end of June, the streets during the first weeks of July took on an air of eerie quiet. It was as if the city had gone on holiday. But behind this façade, many people were busily preparing to 'bring on' the Games.

After the years of planning, the Games were now arriving! But would the city cope? Would the plans for getting people to and from venues, for them to enjoy the sports and participate in the cultural activities be appropriate? Would the citizens of Glasgow have the opportunity to be involved? Would the volunteers be ready to help out the staff in the OC and the Council and its partners?

So many questions, all being answered, as we now know, with an emphatic YES. Record numbers of tickets were sold, more people travelled into and through Glasgow than ever before on public transport, the railways across the country carried more passengers than at any point in Scotland's railway history, and the hotels and guesthouse accommodation recorded levels of occupancy as high as 95% or more. And above all else, hundreds of thousands of people were thronging the streets, parks and sporting venues across the city, creating an atmosphere of celebration and festivity, from early morning to late at night. Even the notoriously erratic Glasgow weather added its own heat to the first few days when Glasgow buzzed.

To achieve this required a major coordinated operation, one of the largest seen in the city and Scotland – and one that at times tested the systems close to breaking point!

Business as usual?

One of the themes which ran through the planning and preparation for the XX Commonwealth Games for the City Council was the desire to connect them with the normal business of the Council and with the normal lives of Glaswegians and Scots. This had been at the centre of the legacy planning (Chapter 5) ensuring that the Games had a positive impact on the city. But 'business as usual' was also a necessary element to the Council's approach to management of the Games. Despite the public focus on the Games, many parts of the city had to continue to function as normal, providing services and support to citizens and businesses.

To help achieve this continuity, services and functions of the Council viewed the Commonwealth Games as just 'another event'. The experience of organising major events and festivals over the years gave many of those involved expertise and knowledge to draw upon. For the managers and teams within the Games venues, such as the Emirates and Scotstoun, their approach to the Games was shaped by years of experience of hosting large scale events, albeit in a single sport. The city operations teams responsible for safety, for cleansing and for transport each had considerable experience in delivering support for an event – whether for a major cultural concert, an international football match, or the annual Great Scottish Run.

But the Commonwealth Games was of course not really 'business as usual'. Its impact on the city was of a scale that was inevitably difficult to plan for. Combining 17 international sporting events into one, over 12 days, and then hosting a fortnight of cultural events at the same time was never going to be the same as anything the city and Council family staff had experienced before. And there was the additional complexity of working together effectively with the Organising Committee and many agencies from across Scotland.

As the Games approached, responsibility for some aspects of the planning gradually moved away from the Council and became more focused on the OC. The final preparation of the sports venues and the organisation of the Athletes' Village moved from being the Council's responsibility to the OC's as Games venues were fitted out for athletes, officials and spectators and new contracts were arranged for cleaning and the myriad of other tasks which are required to allow events to run smoothly.

There were also key roles for national agencies. On behalf of the
Scottish Government, Police Scotland had overall responsibility for
security, led by Deputy Chief Constable Steve Allan. As well as planning the use of their own resources, his team coordinated the involvement of the armed forces, the Scottish Prison Service and private
security contractors who all provided personnel. Agencies such as
Transport Scotland worked alongside ScotRail, the national rail operator, and contractors to plan for travelling into and out of Glasgow,
whilst First Bus coordinated bus services within the city.

In parallel, the Council family had responsibility for preparing the
Festival 2014 sites at Glasgow Green, the Merchant City and Kelvingrove Park and for the spaces between the venues. While many staff
continued to work on 'business as usual' - including a roster of senior
staff - most senior staff at Glasgow Life, coordinating the Festival 2014
activities, and the Council's city operations team leaders, increasingly found this formed a smaller and smaller proportion of their day
jobs. This was led from the top, with the Council's Chief Executive
George Black, devoting all of his attention to overseeing the Council's
role in getting the city ready. Similar experiences were present in
many of the Council departments as senior staff focused not only on
the organisation of their contributions but also on how these came together to present the city to the expected visitors. There was a sense
of urgency - and a definite endpoint, as well as a collective desire to
make the most of the opportunity.

But alongside this, services across the city continued to function
with as little disruption as possible. Bins were emptied, vulnerable
people were supported by social workers, the city parks continued to
be maintained and, on the streets, transport continued to be provided. Alternative sport and fitness centres such as the super-gyms at
Bellahouston and the Gorbals offered opportunities for residents to
continue to attend classes and use facilities throughout Games time.

Dressing the city

In late 2013, with the SSE Hydro and the Athletes' village completed and the Queen's Baton Relay launched by the Queen at Buckingham Palace, there was a sense amongst the Glasgow partners that planning was progressing well. The CGF coordination committee who monitor progress had reported favourably on progress and most of the essential building blocks – venues, transport systems, volunteers, sports programme, athlete selection, ticket sales – were in place. The report card presented at coordinating meetings in late 2013 could aptly have been summed up as the 2014 Games would be delivered competently, on time, on budget, as promised.

Did you know?
More than 37,000 m² of public realm in and around the city centre were enhanced in the lead up to the Games by the City Council.

There had been much pressure to achieve this, but now there was a renewed and fresh sense of greater possibilities – the chance to generate 'the best games ever'. Spurred on by George Black and David Grevemberg, the City Council working in collaboration with the OC took the lead to ensure that the city's 'look' was one that inspired people to be part of the celebrations. They wanted to create a welcoming, safe and fun environment for visitors and residents within the public spaces across the city.

The decision to allocate part of the budget towards this offered opportunities to build upon the work already planned and to undertake additional projects and initiatives. A programme of work was rolled out to help make the city look its best. As well as preparing the very visible and colourful banners that adorned the main routes in and through the city and at all the transport hubs, in George Square the 'Big G' was unveiled at the end of May and became one of the most photographed parts of the Games.

Work had already brought about changes in the city. Between the city centre and the main Games venues, the Council team undertook a programme of improvements in key sites that formed main Games routes. New surfaces and greenery were provided along the Clyde at Anderston Quay, Lancefield Quay, Custom House Quay Gardens and along the Kelvin Walkway/Eldon Street underpass at Kelvingrove Park. Spaces alongside the new paths and cycle routes between the

Emirates Arena and Bridgeton and Glasgow Green were landscaped. Additionally alongside the 'look' programme, Glasgow City Council undertook a wayfinding programme helping people navigate their way around the city. Purple signs marked out the Games time transport routes for those providing official transport, whilst green signs on lamp-posts and on pavements helped to guide cyclists and walkers – usefully including an indication of the time to get to the city centre or to venues by each mode of travel.

Did you know?
The Barras market has for more than 100 years been a thriving part of the East End of the city, originally where hawkers sold from their handcart or 'barras'.

In other parts of the city, attention was given by Land & Environment Services (LES) to adding floral displays in local communities and in the city's many parks, and in communities such as Calton where the world famous Barras market is located, an action plan that had been developed to improve open spaces and arts projects created to freshen up the area. And in the days before the start of the Games, many individual households added their own bunting, flags and other decorations as celebration of the Games or particular nations.

Not all the improvements and their future use were welcomed by everyone. The demolition of the B-listed London Road School outside Celtic Park after years of uncertainty about its future generated some concern over the loss of an architectural feature of the area, but exhaustive searches for other uses for the building had already been pursued. More controversial has been temporary nature of the Barrowland Park. Costing more than £600,000, the park has as its centrepiece The Album Pathway, a specially commissioned artwork, supported by Velocity and listing every band that has played at the famous nearby Barrowlands. Although the park was planned to be temporary and the site redeveloped with the Album Pathway retained and relocated elsewhere in the city, local residents have appreciated the local public space and are now campaigning for its retention.

Recycling the refuse, cleaning the stage

The Council set the ambitious target of ensuring that 80% of the waste associated with the Games that would previously have gone to landfill was diverted to be either recycled or reused. To help achieve this and to meet the sustainability objectives set out in the bid, all partners had key roles to play in how they awarded contracts.

The OC for example developed its own sustainability procurement policy which allowed it to monitor waste and other sustainability measures from its contractors and this helped to encourage all the businesses involved in the Games to think about packaging, waste and transportation.

Priority had been given in the preparation of the Games to include designing and building venues using recycled and reclaimed materials where possible – such as in the Athletes' Village and in the refurbishment of Tollcross – and to minimise waste during construction. At Games time, efforts were made to decrease the amount of secondary and tertiary packaging (the additional layers of wrapping to hold units together) and to ensure that most packaging could be recycled and, where possible was already made from recycled material. Zero Waste principles were applied to contracts to help achieve this and to ensure that contractors were aware of the expectations of them as suppliers.

Within the Council, Land and Environment Services and Glasgow Life, with the support of other organisations such as Zero Waste Scotland, were involved in a major campaign during the Games and the associated Festival 2014 to encourage people to separate their refuse. 80 volunteer 'recycling ambassadors' from Zero Waste Scotland were at Glasgow Green Live Zone to help this process and to distribute information to encourage residents and visitors to continue to separate waste. The volunteers included students, members of the public and employees from both Zero Waste Scotland and the waste managers Viridor.

Did you know?
Household food waste, collected and responsibly recycled by householders all across the west of Scotland, was turned via composting into the turf laid at the Athletes' Village.

Like this project, the focus during the Games on reducing waste, reusing and recycling and thus minimising waste that goes to land-fill was viewed as a demonstration of what is possible across the city. Learning from this experience, the Council's LES department aims to extend the target achieved during the Games to the regular management of waste across the city.

Piloting emission reduction

However, not all aspects of sustainability were as easily achieved or indeed managed. One of these – the creation of low emission zones around the venue areas – was only partially successful and as the Games approached the aspirational targets were dropped.

The idea of reducing emissions from vehicles in order to provide a cleaner environment is challenging when, like most cities, there is a steady rise in the number of vehicles on the roads, and a continuing demand from residents and businesses to have access to vehicles. Engineering redesign of engines and more efficient and effective vehicle emission controls are making a difference but other actions may be needed to provide clean air.

During the Games, Glasgow City Council with the support of the OC had been piloting the idea of low emission zones (LEZs). The intention had been to create such zones by restricting access to areas around Games venues for all but low emission vehicles. This was to be supported by the use of modern public transport and service vehicles with the highest specification of emission reduction. The inclusion of free public transport in Games tickets and the encouragement of active travel – with cycle park areas and safe walk routes marked – were also designed to help generate LEZs.

For the City Council, the Games plan provided the opportunity to undertake a pilot project to test the extent to which LEZs might be a viable option for the future in Glasgow and other cities.

In early July 2014, however, the pilot scheme was amended as it became evident that achieving the desired levels of emission around each venue was not possible given the available vehicles. Under the revised scheme, the LEZ was restricted to only those areas within the security cordon at each venue. This meant that the only vehicles having to comply were those providing transport for athletes and officials, special needs transport and the support services – a much more restricted list than originally planned.

In part this amendment reflected the difficulty of sourcing suf
ficient public transport meeting low emission standards. Although
new, low emission buses and cars were used to transport athletes and
officials into the zones, other buses used to transport spectators outside of the zone were not of the same emission standard, and many of
the additional fleet added to meet extra demand were of lower standards. As a result the applicability of the lessons learnt from the test to
other parts of the city were limited.

Accommodating visitors

To say that Glasgow reached capacity during the Commonwealth
Games may be a slight exaggeration. Certainly the long and patient
queues which formed to gain access to the Festival venues and Live
Zones during most of the 12 days illustrated the pressures involved.
But perhaps the best indicator of the city's capacity was the record
figure of 95.3% occupancy rate in the city's hotels and similar levels in
guesthouses. Even with the growth in capacity in the city hotel space
in the last 10 years, this was an all-time record.

But one consequence of this was the wider net cast by those looking for available and affordable accommodation around Games time.
Many sought out hotels and guesthouses in Stirling and Edinburgh
or in Ayrshire where direct journeys into the city by public transport
were possible. Occupancy rates in these places all rose with significant increases across Scotland in hostels as well as rates of 70% and
82% for self-catering and hotels respectively, all helping to boost
tourism across Scotland.

In contrast to the experience in previous major sporting events, including the experience of London at the time of the 2012 Olympics, across Glasgow businesses experienced a growth in activity even during the Games. Within the city, there was an increase in shoppers of about 36% from the previous year whilst across all of Scotland's high street, retail figures show a 22% rise in shoppers from the same time in 2013 and across the city restaurants and bars experienced high demand as visitors and residents enjoyed the sporting and cultural festivities.

Getting us there and back

The greatest challenge presented by an event of this size and complexity comes in planning how to get people to and from venues – and into and out of the city. Whilst ticket sales – and the location of the sales – give a broad picture of spectators for these events, a feature of the Glasgow Commonwealth Games was the large number of opportunities available free and unticketed each day. In addition to the 1.3 million tickets for the Games venues, the Glasgow Green Live Zone site attracted more than 384,000 attendances, whilst the Merchant City Live Zone and the BBC @ The Quay together had an average of 34,000 attendances per day.

Preparing for this large flow into and through the city was a complex logistical task, and involved national and local agencies alongside the OC and the City Council.

Some elements of the transport planning were priorities and worked very efficiently. Glasgow set out its intention in its bid document that athletes would be able to get to most venues within the Glasgow area within 20 minutes travel from the Athletes' Village. To achieve this, routeways across the city were marked out as part of the Games Route Networks (GRN) and in key areas Games specific lanes were created to enable movement for athletes and officials, with dedicated buses and a fleet of cars provided to get teams to venues. Months of planning, many rehearsals and familiarisation journeys for the Clydesiders driving the cars and the professional bus drivers enabled this GRN to work successfully. 97% of all journeys took less than 20 minutes.

Other aspects of travel movement were more difficult to predict. One of the lessons learnt at Manchester 2002 in relation to transport was the importance of having a single coordination body with local knowledge to lead the delivery of transport. At the 2002 Games, the City Council and the OC took the decision to get the local public transport agency, Greater Manchester Public Transport Executive (GMPTE), involved in a long-term relationship and they used the GMPTE expertise to lead transport planning.

In the absence of a similar regional transport body in Glasgow, roles and responsibilities were split although brought together through a coordinating centre at Games time. In planning journeys by road into Glasgow from outside the city and across Scotland, the national agency, Transport Scotland, took the lead. Working with its contractors they focused on the provision of information and advice about getting to Glasgow using the main motorways and arterial routes. In the months leading up to the Games on July 23rd, across the motorway network, variable road signs were used to warn commuters and drivers that they needed to prepare for their journeys during the time of the Games. This was supported by the Get Ready Glasgow campaign which was designed to help residents and businesses across the city prepare for the Games. With live updates online and by twitter, the services aimed to provide information on council services and security as well as transport and travel. Emphasis was placed on re-timing (especially of journeys into and through the city), re-moding (between transport options), re-routing and reducing the need to travel.

Supported by the mobile apps, website information and call centre help, the approach worked effectively with about 90% of all strategic motorway journeys across the city taking no more than 5% longer than normal.

For rail travel, ScotRail, who ran the franchise for most of the rail services in Scotland, had a more difficult challenge. Not only had they to plan for inter-city journeys into Glasgow, but within the city they had to get passengers from the city centre to the three main venue clusters using the commuter network. Passenger flow management systems were put in place on the main east-west link between Dalmarnock (the nearest station for the Emirates Arena and Celtic Park) and the SECC precinct at Exhibition Centre station. And high capacity trains were used to link Central Station with the Hampden Park venue for the athletics and the closing ceremony through Mount Florida station.

More than 150,000 journeys were made each day to the venue stations and more than 3.5 million people passed through the city's Central Station during the Games, making the railway network the busiest it has ever been. Contingency planning had meant that ScotRail had brought in extra staff, including under an apprenticeship scheme, to help marshall travellers at each station. They also had queue management systems.

High demand for later services on key nights was expected on the longer distance routes to other Scottish cities from Queen Street station, with longer and more frequent trains timetabled to run between Glasgow and Edinburgh. However, even these plans had to be adjusted in the first few days as demand outstripped capacity from early morning onwards. Emergency planning meetings on the first evening of the Games resulted in a change to ScotRail's plans. With support from Police Scotland and British Transport Police, passenger management at the main stations was put in place and more trains were brought into service in the late evenings as planned timetable changes were ditched. Every train available – including those hired in by ScotRail to complement the usual rolling stock – was in use and schedules were adjusted to include more stations on the busiest routes.

For most spectators and travellers, despite the need to queue and disruption to the normal service timetables, the planning for the Games time use of the rail network and trunk road network was effective. The flexible and responsive approach adopted by the station teams enabled most people to reach destinations in time for events and to return home or to hotels. And commuters and other road users heeded the advice to be flexible in their travel plans.

Within Glasgow, the preparation of travel plans was less smooth. In contrast to the many other aspects of the preparation for the Games that were in place, by April 2014 the transport plans had not been finalised. Initial planning had gone well and there was a degree of confidence in the team coordinating planning that everything would come together.

To oversee and coordinate transport for the city during the Games, a Glasgow 2014 transport coordination group was formed in the early stages of the Games preparation. This brought together teams from the OC and a team from Land and Environmental Services from the City Council, with shared leadership. They had jointly published the first version of the Transport Plan for the city in September 2010, preparing the process of planning ahead so that disruption in the city could be minimised. The 2010 plan indicated that it would be a 'live document' being updated throughout the planning and delivery period with two further versions to be published prior to 2014.

In fact, the updated Transport Strategic Plan was eventually published by the coordination team in April 2014, but even then detailed information and advice on transport was limited. A number of factors contributed to this.

First, the coordination team was using a transport modelling approach which required information on the origins and destination of each ticket holder to plan transport needs. Delays in getting this together for the 1.3m ticket holders and a late rush in sales of tickets meant that accurate and up to date information was not available. In addition, no information was known about where each ticket holder was staying during the Games and thus how they would arrive into the city. This meant that planning capacity was imprecise and travel management relied on information on the day.

Second, providing a system of park and ride facilities on the edge of the city to reduce car travel in the city was developed late in the planning process. Negotiations to acquire use of the sites and the logistics of transporting spectators to and from them and the venues by bus were still continuing in the months leading up to the Games. Eventually in early June 2014, 8000 places were secured, including Hamilton International Park, Eurocentral, and Baldinnie Park to the east, Silverburn and Freescale in East Kilbride to the south, and Blochairn to the north, each servicing different venues. With each person having to book both a ticket and a time slot in which to arrive, the system offered a regulated way of managing this demand and should have allowed planning of the resources necessary at any point in advance of the event.

Did you know?
The Park + Ride ticket system used for the Games – ticketSOUP – is run by the Scottish Exhibition and Conference Centre?

Third, the appointment of a transport sponsor for the Games was made late. In their desire to gain support from the best sponsor, the OC finalised sponsorship arrangements with First Bus in May 2014. They took on the role of coordinating bus provision for spectators as well as the provision of transport for the Games workforce and athletes. With only two months to plan the logistics, First Bus was under pressure to secure sufficient vehicles and capacity and to undertake the necessary driver training.

But perhaps most important was that the approach to transport planning was untested. Unlike other aspects of the Games, no one in Glasgow had experience of planning and providing for the number of people who were to descend on the city and at no point previously had the transport systems in the city had to cope with this level of demand. The city's experience was limited to planning for a single major event at one venue where timing and journey plans of arrivals and departures were more certain.

Together these factors resulted in problems in the first few days of the Games. On the first evening at the end of the opening ceremony the lack of past experience of managing large numbers across the city became evident. Despite having sufficient capacity available, poor management of flows meant that spectators were walking through the bus turning and loading areas, disrupting schedules. But the main issues emerged on the first Saturday when the athletics programme at Hampden started in what was an already busy schedule of events. For those catching the free bus shuttle service from the city centre to Hampden, the lack of time to prepare bus drivers became evident. These shuttle services had been sub-contracted to Stagecoach by First Bus, and the bus fleet and drivers were on loan from cities across the UK. Unfamiliar with Glasgow and lacking training on routes, some of the bus drivers had to rely on local passengers for directions. And at Hampden poor planning of drop-off points meant that buses returning to the city centre cut across oncoming Games traffic.

Other spectators using the park and ride facilities, especially at Silverburn, found that the shuttle service of buses was unable to cope. Early arrivals – heeding the message of adding extra time for journeys – and insufficient bus capacity resulted in delays of up to 2 hours.

Did you know?
During the Games the new Glasgow Operation Centre at Eastgate in the East End of the city coordinated traffic management, bringing together teams from ScotRail, Transport Scotland, FirstBus and Police Scotland as well as Community Safety Glasgow.

However, one of the strengths of the coordinated transport planning approach was the ability to respond quickly to such issues. The lessons were quickly learnt. After the first day, the park and ride scheme worked efficiently with additional bus capacity being hired to ensure everyone arrived in time for events. For the city centre shuttle services, additional staff were brought in to accompany drivers to ensure they became familiar with routes, and at venues alternative drop off and pick up points were allocated to allow more for efficient and effective services.

Coordinating the City

In contrast to these visible signs that Glasgow was hosting the Games, behind the scenes a major team of staff from the Council, from Police Scotland, from transport agencies, and the OC were working together to ensure that all the city operations went smoothly.

Based on an incident and emergency response model, the Command, Co-ordination and Communication structure (C3, as it was referred to) was the means by which the Council and its partners were able to manage activity during the Games. Reporting to the overall command or Games Executive Team lead by the Council Chief Executive George Black, the C3 structure was designed to allow both the central coordination of all relevant information and the cascading of the necessary information to different groups. It has proven to be effective and adaptable, and is likely to be the model used in future by the City Council and other partners in planning for major incidents and disasters.

The C3 teams were based in the City Council's Eastgate premises, one of the most advanced control centres in Europe equipped with screens showing images from all CCTV cameras in the city, high tech telecommunication equipment and bringing together police and civilian teams. Normally the Eastgate centre handles community safety issues for Glasgow, staffed by Community Safety Glasgow and Police Scotland, and their expertise was invaluable in helping the City Operations for the Games.

The success of the C3 structure was that there were no major or emergency incidents to be dealt with during the fortnight of the Games.

Using the Games' experiences in future

Until a host city experiences the challenge of hosting a major sporting event of the scale of the Games, planning for it will always be a challenge. For Glasgow, most aspects of the preparation and planning went well – and remained below the public radar. In one of the largest security operations in the city, for example, the preparation meant that there were no major security issues during the Games with the huge commitment required by Police Scotland ensuring the events across the city passed safely. Other aspects had been well tested through prior experience, including the use of venues for major events over the preceding years. But in some respects, and in the case of Glasgow this was primarily in relation to transport, learning has to take place during the event.

With the city experiencing its largest ever influx of visitors, doubling its size on the first weekend of the Games, planning any operation to 'bring it on' was always going to be stretched. The test for any host city is thus not only to get people to venues and to enjoy the Games – and 97% of spectators were satisfied or very satisfied and 74% satisfied with their overall journey experience – but to be able to adapt to the changing patterns of demand. Unseen by almost everyone, the sophisticated command, coordination and communication structures put in place to respond to needs was viewed as a success. The multi-agency approach and the readiness planning that had been organised in advance provided not only rapid response but allowed for effective cascading and sharing of information. For the City Council, this system will be a legacy from the Games as it becomes part of the Council's plans to be able to respond to major events as well as incidents and emergencies in the future, and helps as it develops its systems as a 'resilient city'.

More visibly, a testament to the hours of effort by staff across the city and beyond to deliver the plans was the inclusion of a parade of 220 representatives of some of the services during the closing ceremony, a reminder of the valuable roles they had played in ensuring that the Games and the related activity across the city had been delivered successfully.

Image 124:
Scotland's Craig
Howieson Playing
Srilankan Dinesh
Deshappriya,
Table Tennis

Image 125:
Men's Judo – 60kg
Category Bronze Medal
Winner John Buchanan
of Team Scotland
celebrates, the SECC

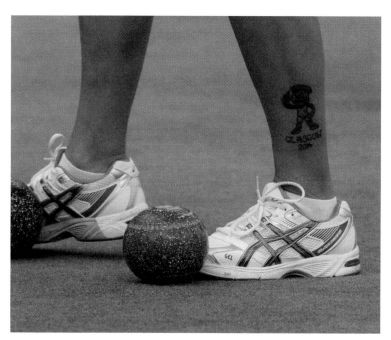

Image 126:
A Scotland Fan at
Hampden

Image 127:
The Tattoo of Clyde
on the Leg of Lorraine
Molloy, Kelvingrove
Lawn Bowls

Image 128:
Ross Murdoch
Competes in the Men's
50m Breaststroke
Semifinal, Tollcross
International Swimming
Centre

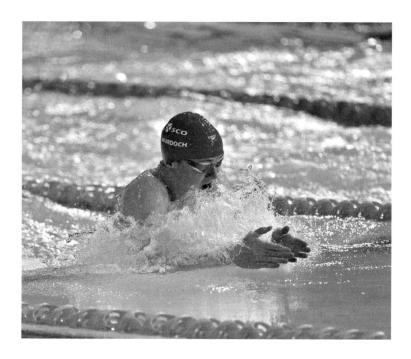

Glasgow's Commonwealth Games: behind the scenes

"Festival 2014, the largest ever cultural event connected with the Games sought not only to reinforce the ideals of the Commonwealth Games but also a chance to connect communities in the city with the Commonwealth"

Chapter 8
Games time city

With the arrival of more than 4,500 athletes to Glasgow and the opening of the Games with its traditional parade of the 71 nations and territories taking part, much of the world's attention was focused on the sporting endeavours which followed. The quest for world and Commonwealth records, for medals and for personal best performances inevitably means that sport takes centre stage. But amidst the enormous buzz and excitement that accompanied the sporting events during the Games in Glasgow, it was easy for anyone not in the city during the Games to be unaware of the other ways in which this sporting event was connecting with the place.

Glasgow sought to ensure that the Games made connections beyond the venues, providing a more integrated programme of cultural events, more opportunities to bring the Games into communities, and making more visible the values that underpin the Commonwealth Games. With the cultural programme attracting hundreds of thousands of visitors, with thousands lining the streets for events and with many taking part in the other activities, these other activities were an important part of defining the character of 'Game time city' as one that sought to be inclusive.

Marathon tussles
The marathon – like the road cycling events – provides an opportunity for sport to move away from specific venues and become a community event. As one of the main unticketed events of the Games, the marathon provides one of the few opportunities within the Games for anyone across the city to be spectators. But the event is also a key competition and like other sporting aspects of the Games has its own requirements.

On Sunday 26 July, elite female and male athletes took part in the Commonwealth Games marathon, on a route which took the runners from Glasgow Green through the heart of the city and then out to the southern parks at Bellahouston and Pollok before returning through the Gorbals to the Green. The two lap race enabled good spectator vantage points with much of the route lined with thousands of supporters and with many crossing between points to see their favoured runners. The route also provided positive television coverage of the city's landmarks, incorporating vistas of many of the Games venues.

Selecting this route however proved to be a point of tension, illustrating some of the competing desires and priorities between the City Council and the OC.

For the OC, in the context of its declared intention to provide an 'athlete centred Games', the desire was understandably to provide a fast, flat course which offered the athletes the ideal opportunity to achieve their best times, to offer maximum links with the main Games venues and be easier to keep secure. Their proposed route thus incorporated the flat areas on the side of the River Clyde, taking the athletes west to the venue clusters at the SECC and Scotstoun and east to the Emirates Arena at Dalmarnock. Much of this route was easily managed as it crossed through few communities and residential areas. And it was technically suitable for television coverage of the event.

The leadership from the Glasgow partners were adamant that with an international television audience of millions the marathon offered the opportunity to showcase key landmarks and sites in the city as the runners progressed along the route. For them the inclusion of George Square at the heart of the city, the Merchant City where cultural events were to be held, the Clyde waterfront, and the parklands of the city had to be key elements of a route. And in addition they wanted to ensure that the route was closer to communities within the city, passing through areas where people lived rather than bypassing them as the OC route would do.

Importantly too, the Glasgow partners had local experience in delivering an event of this type and scale. Each year, they organised Scotland's largest race, the Great Scottish Run, which, although a half marathon, was renowned as a fast(ish), scenic course which attracted many spectators. And it was held on a route which included both the city centre and communities to the southwest of the city. As well as providing security, one of the features of the Great Scottish Run was the support and involvement of local communities who cheered and supported runners as they passed along the residential streets.

Months of negotiation saw several iterations of courses being proposed and then rejected and after interventions from the civic leaders, the central argument of a route which showcased the character of the city of Glasgow won the argument.

Despite these preceding differences, the success of the marathon route for the runners and the spectators - as well as the television audience - was clear. Huge crowds lined almost the entire route, offering the atmosphere of a major city marathon. And despite the course not being very flat, some athletes were able to achieve their personal best times, including Jessica Trengove from Australia who won bronze in the women's race and Michael Shelley (Australia) who won the men's race. Importantly the marathon - like the cycling road races - brought the Games into communities beyond those around the main venues and enabled them to turn the event into local festivals.

Clyde Mascot and the trail

Beyond the more formal and obvious 'festival' focus of the Cultural Programme (see below), the Council engaged with more quirky ways to engender a feeling of connection between the Games and the city - one that would appeal both to residents and visitors.

The 'thistle man' mascot Clyde caught the public imagination since its (or is that his?) launch in September 2012. Designed by Beth Gilmour from Cumbernauld and given life by creative digital consultants Nerv, it was originally designed for young people. However, as was evident during the Games, the appeal of the Clyde toy spanned all ages. Across the venues people young and older were seen clutching their Clyde toy, and it became one of the enduring images of the Games. More than 126,000 Clyde toys were sold - the entire stock - and a pre-order scheme after the Games was put in place to enable disappointed customers to get their mascot for Christmas 2014.

Prior to the Games, children and young people in Glasgow were asked to come up with a range of new outfits for Clyde as part of a legacy project run earlier in the year by Glasgow City Council and Glasgow 2014 in partnership with children's charity UNICEF. Pupils from Glasgow's nurseries, primary and secondary schools were invited to submit designs inspired by the city itself.

Using these designs, a trail – Clyde's Trail – was made up of 25 unique, 'life-sized' fibreglass statues of the Games mascot, located across Glasgow throughout the Games, many close to venues but others marking transects between communities or along key walkways like the River Clyde. With the encouragement to take 'selfies' and record the counting of each Clyde (using the QR codes) this trail was a popular way to visit different parts of the city and navigate between venues – and proved a great way to encourage visitors and residents to walk further.

Adding an app (or two)

Whilst the Clyde Trail offered a chance to navigate round the city centre and surrounding areas close to the Games venues, other ways of helping the influx of visitors unfamiliar with the city – and even residents unfamiliar with parts of the city – to find their way about and to gain more insights and information about the city were developed for the Games using mobile technologies. Indeed, as a catalyst, the Games encouraged companies and others to look afresh at how they provide public information across the city, and new ways of providing accurate and up to date data were progressed more quickly.

Travel information sources were greatly expanded. Traveline Scotland and Traffic Scotland launched a new free iPhone app in advance of the Games to provide information to help plan journeys in the Greater Glasgow area. Including transport departure boards and journey planner options, the aim was to help reinforce the message of planning journeys in advance. Along with its website and customer call centre which also provided regular updates on travel flows, they helped more than 900,000 journeys to be planned.

Within the Glasgow area, First Bus, the largest bus operator in the city and one of the supporters of the Games, also offered a free download of their app providing timetable information, service updates and maps relating to the city's largest bus operator. And during the Games, First Glasgow also announced the start of its mticket app, allowing customers to get bus tickets sent to their mobile phones.

Beyond transport, a series of mobile apps were developed

specifically around the Games to provide information connected with venues and the events programmes, and about the sights of the city. One of these was created for the OC. Its My Games app not only provided information on the venues and the sporting calendars but also on exploring the city between venues. It was downloaded onto over 460,000 devices in the period of the Games and augmented the more traditional ways of navigating across the city. One million maps were handed out to many by the Host City Volunteers.

One of the more imaginative and award-winning apps linked to the Games was created as a Games legacy research project. Developed by a team from the Universities of Glasgow and Strathclyde, the MyCityApp was also available before and during the Games. This sought to encourage users to engage in greater levels of physical activity, using the app not only to provide information on sights and venues but also offering 'rewards' based on the amount of physical activity involved in the daily patterns of movement. With goals set both in terms of personal achievements and more competitively in comparison with others, the project demonstrated how mobile technologies can support the wider legacy message of the Games to improve health and wellbeing.

Creating the 'festival effect'

For most people in the city during the Games the highlight beyond the sport was the cultural programme, Festival 2014. This largest ever cultural event connected with the Games sought not only to reinforce the ideals of the Commonwealth Games but also a chance to connect communities in the city and across Scotland with the Games and the Commonwealth.

Did you know?
The Cultural Programme was proposed to create a 'live city' – where activities and events would appeal to people who had limited interest in sport and who could benefit from being part of the festival.

And there was a desire to use these cultural events to engender the creation of a sense of community involvement in the sporting occasion, what is termed the 'festival effect'. Football fans will recognise this sense of shared attachment which can emerge when their team is performing well, with their sense of belonging not just being to the club but also to the town or community. Such festival effects are rather ephemeral, connected with the success of the team, the performances by athletes, or the event itself – and difficult to capture and build upon.

The evidence from previous major events suggests that the 'festival effect' can encourage people to think about becoming more active through informal celebrations in their own communities and become more involved in pursuits in which they are already interested without having to think of them as being exercise or getting healthy.

Engendering a 'festival effect' from the Glasgow 2014 Cultural Programme of events was coordinated jointly by Creative Scotland, the national agency for art and culture in Scotland, and Glasgow Life within the city.

> **Did you know?**
> The Cultural Programme, including the nationwide Culture 2014 and the Glasgow based Festival 2014, was the most ambitious cultural celebration ever held in Scotland. 1,500 events took place across the country, including 250 associated with the Queen's Baton Relay.

A total of £4m was made available to support groups and communities across Scotland to create projects inspired by the Commonwealth Games. As part of the year-long programme, some of the 150 events involved existing larger culture and arts organisations but many were local productions and events where the inspiration was the Games, and the desire was to be part of the celebrations. And for most the purpose was to create an opportunity for local communities to show how the values of the Commonwealth and the Games were resonating with them.

In Glasgow, the focus was on the few weeks immediately leading up to and during the Games. Events were held across the city's arts and culture venues, in clubs, in the city's parks and in the Live Zones. The programme was varied – from the dance festival Gathered Together in Tramway to a mixed programme of acts in Richmond Park in the Gorbals as part of the East End Series. Some involved many people and some only a few, and included music, art and comedy as well as others with more of a party atmosphere.

One of the larger and more formal contributions to Festival 2014 was by the National Theatre of Scotland. Their production of the Tin Forest was for many visitors one of the highlights. Unrelated to sport, the Tin Forest sought to make connections between culture, creative art and Glasgow's history, but a key part of the performance was that it required these connections to be developed by people themselves.

Drawing on the work of children's author Helen Ward and illustrator Wayne Anderson, the Tin Forest was a celebration of the city's industrial past and provided participants the chance to imagine its creative future. Initially drawing on four of Glasgow's ex-industrial communities – Springburn, the East End, Govan and Southwest Glasgow – the production has collected stories, dream and wishes from communities. During the Commonwealth Games, the (previously derelict) South Rotunda on the banks of the Clyde was transformed into a set of rooms through which groups of participants journeyed to see the dreams and the magical but odd world built by a wee crabbit man guided by eccentric puppets and bampots.

More than 8,700 attended the Tin Forest, including 1,000 at the International presentation in Springburn and Glasgow Green which involved 90 young people from across the Commonwealth and Scotland ahead of the Games. The Games time venue at the transformed South Rotunda – part of Glasgow's heritage – attracted over 6,300.

Altogether, Festival 2014 was the biggest party Glasgow has ever organised. Featuring theatre, dance, music, visual arts, comedy and multi-media events, the Festival was held in venues across the city, extending well beyond the large theatres and cinemas into local community centres and public spaces.

The centrepiece was three specially designed 'live zones' at Glasgow Green and in the extended Merchant City Festival – both at the heart of the city – and at the Kelvingrove Bandstand in the West End. Except for the opening and closing ceremonies, these venues were open free to the public, and attracted tens of thousands of visitors every day. Even the summer drizzle and rain during the Games did not dampen the spirits of those who came along – to follow the sporting action on the big screens, to watch dance and comedy shows, listen to the live acts or take part in the fun events available.

Did you know?
Festival 2014 attracted 852,794 attendances, including 384,199 at Glasgow Green, 213,350 in the Merchant City and 29,732 at the Kelvingrove Bandstand.

The Merchant City Festival is an annual event held within the precincts of the recently regenerated area in the city centre and host to many parts of Glasgow's cultural sector. The festival is a celebration of multi-culturalism and is usually held in the last week of the month of July. For the Games it was extended to last 3 weeks and expanded to cover almost the entire Merchant City area.

Whilst Glasgow Green and the Merchant City locations had the largest attendances, to the west at Kelvingrove Park, the third venue was a key and new part of Festival 2014. The re-opened and refurbished Kelvingrove Bandstand and Amphitheatre was symbolically a key part of the cultural legacy of the Games.

Having been closed in 1999 and falling into a state of disrepair, the bandstand had become the focus of considerable public concern about its neglect and many calls for the City Council to take action. Despite a number of proposals emerging, none had been taken forward to provide a sustainable future for the site. The decision taken by City Council to refurbish this and make it a feature of the cultural programme was thus symbolically important.

Image 129:
Kelvingrove Bandstand
– at the Heart of the
Live Zone

Did you know?
To save the Kelvingrove Bandstand a partnership was formed between the City Council, Glasgow Life and Glasgow Building Preservation Trust. Funding of £2.1m, including a grant from the Heritage Lottery Fund, was made available to refurbish it, including the addition of a platform lift.

The only remaining bandstand in Glasgow and one of only three in Scotland with its own amphitheatre, the venue offered an excellent open air site for cultural activities during the Games and proved a popular location for families in Festival 2014. And in the weeks following the Bandstand hosted some of the mainstream Scottish acts (such as Squeeze and Capercaillie) as well as emerging acts, with ticket sales helping to secure it as one of Glasgow's new (or renewed) cultural venues!

Organising the 2014 Cultural Programme was a significant undertaking requiring national and local partners to work together. When conceived and planned in the early stages of the bid, the original intention was to have the cultural programme coordinated alongside the Queen's Baton Relay and the opening and closing ceremonies by a dedicated person within the OC. However, an appointment of a director within the OC was not made and, to fill this vacuum, Bridget McConnell from Glasgow Life took on this role along with Jill Miller, Director of Cultural Services.

This created both benefits and drawbacks. The separation from the OC created a benefit, enabling Glasgow Life to bring Creative Scotland, the national agency supporting arts and creative industries into the development of the cultural programme. Together they brought to life a more ambitious programme of cultural events than had been associated with previous Commonwealth Games – and proved to be one that showed both Scottish and Glasgow character as well as connections directly with the Games and the Commonwealth.

On the other hand, it meant that links between the Cultural programme and the opening and closing ceremonies in the Games were not as easily developed. The OC had outsourced the ceremonies to Jack Morton Worldwide to organise the opening and closing ceremonies and with Glasgow Life also separately developing Festival 2014, relatively limited resources were committed from the OC into making connections. With Glasgow Life having to find their own resources to take forward Festival 2014, considerable effort was required by the senior staff from Glasgow Life to integrate the cultural programme, the ceremonies and the Queen's Baton Relay within Glasgow. Ideally this would have happened earlier than actually occurred, but it was testimony to the team's effort that for those attending the Festival and the Games, this separation was invisible – both were key elements to the creation of the 'festival effect' of the Games.

Equality and the values of the Games

Whilst celebrating the values of the city, the Glasgow partners had indicated in their bid that they wished the Games to provide an opportunity to show too the values of the Commonwealth Games and to assist the development of the Games and the brand.

At the heart of the Commonwealth Games and the work of the CGF are the values of 'humanity, destiny and equality'. These values are what has helped to inspire and unite the millions of people in the Commonwealth and are expected to be demonstrated during the Commonwealth Games. But these are also some of the more contentious aspects of the Commonwealth as there are disagreements within and between nations as to whether their governments uphold such values.

During the Games, conscious efforts were made to celebrate these values, demonstrate their worth and at the same time acknowledge disagreements. The involvement of thousands of people in responding to the UNICEF appeal at the opening ceremony in Glasgow, raising more than £5m though donations made at the time and in the next few days epitomised the humanity and the caring for the destiny of young people. And in the celebrations of sport over the next 11 days, there were many other examples of the values being applied and challenges made when they were not. Protests at the Ugandan government's anti-gay laws occurred alongside the donation of bikes to two Malawian cyclists by the local bike company to enable them to perform better. The donation by the New Zealand team of 30 bikes to the Glasgow charity Bike Station to help them promote mental and physical health through cycling occurred alongside public debate about human rights in Commonwealth nations and territories.

Recognising the importance to demonstrating such values as part of the legacy of the Games, events were held in Glasgow to promote the value of equality. A few days before the start of the Games, the Glasgow City Council, the OC, and Scottish Government broke new ground for a major sport event by hosting an international summit for social change through sport. Organised by Beyond Sport, the session brought together sports and civic leaders to explore the power of the Games to advance promotion of and respect for the Commonwealth Games Federation's core values of humanity, equality and destiny. Speakers included Baroness Tanni Grey-Thompson, former Paralympic gold medal winner, and Sir Craig Reedie (President of the World Anti-Doping Agency), and this reinforced some of the issues raised at the earlier LGBT Human Rights conference in the city addressed by international speakers.

During the Games, LEAP Sports - Leadership, Equality and Active Participation in Sports Scotland - hosted a Pride House in Glasgow including a range of sports, cultural and arts events which shared a common theme, their vision of breaking down the social and personal barriers which discourage LGBT people across the country from participating in Scottish sports. Supported by the City Council and Scottish Government, this legacy project sought to build closer relationships with mainstream sports and, like other parts of the Games time experience, allowed Glasgow not only to set agendas but to use the excitement of the Games to foster new approaches to inclusive sport.

"The best Games ever"

One of the successes of the Glasgow event was the integration of the sporting events with the other activities in the city. This had been identified as part of the original bid to be host city, and reflected the desire to help people across the city and beyond not only celebrate sporting endeavour but to see how sport and culture can together help improve people's lives.

In setting out its plans for the Cultural Programme, Glasgow Life had set out a vision of Glasgow as a 'live city', a place where activities and events would appeal to people even if they had no interest in sport. For most visitors, their experience of the Games was one where all the activities in the city blended into a single celebration and festivity, creating the opportunity to engender the festival effect, and making the Games more inclusive.

The Glasgow experience has also shown how the Games can incorporate new ways of expressing the values of the Commonwealth Games. The inclusion of gay rights debates, a focus on equality (in sport and society) and the partnership with UNICEF all underlined the humanity of the event. Such innovations, as well as the success of the cultural programme, have all assisted in redefining the role of the Commonwealth Games as not only a significant sporting event but also a catalyst for change in the host city and nation, and internationally.

Glasgow has been changed as a result of being the host of the XX Commonwealth Games – and for more than seven years many people in the city have contributed to making sure the 2014 Games are successful in ensuring that such change will continue.

Image 130:
The Lord Provost of
Glasgow Cllr Sadie
Docherty and the
Duchess of Cambridge
meet Clyde

Image 131:
The Duke and Duchess
of Cambridge, and
Prince Harry Greet
Children

Glasgow 's Commonwealth Games: behind the scenes

"The main legacy has been
the boost in confidence
Glasgow has recevied from
being host for the Games.
The experience has helped
leaders across the city to raise
their ambitions"

Chapter 9
Life after the Games

Few who were in Glasgow during the Commonwealth Games will forget the experience. Memories have been created, imaginations of the city reformed, and pride in the city and its people rekindled. Whether in the coming decades people will talk about that moment in Glasgow's history as defining its future, only time will tell. But the Games have certainly left an imprint on the city, both physically and emotionally.

And Glasgow's Commonwealth Games has helped to show how, as a sporting event, it can resonate with so many people and make connections with people through their endeavours. In an era when televised sport and the constant demand for world class performance are dominant - and success is measured in medal hauls - it has been reassuring that other memories have been created. The joy (and dance) of David Katoatau from Kiribati winning his country's first ever Commonwealth Games gold medal at the weightlifting in the SECC precinct's Clyde Auditorium for example more than matched that of Usain Bolt dancing to the Proclaimers ahead of the Jamaican team's Commonwealth Games record performance in the 4 x 400m men's relay!

Glaswegians and the thousands of visitors to the city who came to enjoy a festival of sport and culture showed by their actions that participation in sport at the highest level can be as important as winning. That was the clear message from those watching Uganda play in the Rugby 7s game at Ibrox stadium, or watching the teenager Rosefelo Siosi from the Solomon Islands finish the 5000m at Hampden or seeing the Norfolk Islands playing Australia in the Women's Doubles at badminton in the Emirates Arena. In each case the loudest cheers and overwhelming support was for those who came and took part, representing their country proudly even if they were soundly beaten.

But now that the Games have finished and the baton has formally been handed over to the Gold Coast for the 2018 Games, what next for the city of Glasgow? What is the future for the communities across the city and Scotland touched by the Games?

Moving on... future events

The experience of holding a major sporting event will be put to good use as the city welcomes a wide range of other international sporting events - and other non-sporting events - to Glasgow over the next few years. Each of the main venues in the city will continue to resonate to cheering crowds, encouraging participants in individual sports. And many of these venues will host other events which have been attracted to the city through the investment in modern facilities. The Games were followed quickly with the annual World Pipe Band Championships in August held in Glasgow Green and the annual Great Scottish Run, both drawing in large crowds

The 20th anniversary MTV European Music Awards was held in the SSE Hydro in November 2014, and the World Gymnastics championships will be held there in 2015, when more than 500 gymnasts from 80 nations take part. Also in 2015, the Emirates Arena will host the European Judo Championships, whilst the Tollcross International Swimming Centre will host the IPC (International Paralympic Committee) swimming world championships and three years later the 2018 European Swimming Championships.

The success of the Commonwealth Games has provided other opportunities, including the decision to bring the 2018 European Swimming Championships to the city for the first time. Over the next few years, many national and international events are already committed to use the main sporting venues which housed the Commonwealth Games, generating millions of pounds of activity for the city and Scotland. The legacy of modern, high quality facilities provides a platform for the continuing success of Glasgow's event strategy and provides the standard of facility for training which should help to ensure that the Scottish teams across different sports - not all of them represented at the Commonwealth Games - are able to compete internationally.

The facilities will also continue to be the focus of more local sports development. The National Hockey Centre at Glasgow Green will be at the heart of hockey development at the national level for a sport which has seen growth since the facility opened in late 2013. The Sir Chris Hoy Velodrome, as the home for Scottish Cycling, is already assisting in training an increasing number of people in and around Glasgow who are now participating in track and road cycling.

Image 133:
Women's Gymnastics

Image 134:
Kimberley Renicks,
left and Louise Renicks,
right with their Judo
Gold medals

Moving on... adding facilities

Further investment in sport and culture facilities available for local communities and for national and international visitors is already planned for the coming years. This will enable the momentum from the 2014 Games to be maintained and channelled towards ensuring that Glaswegians are the beneficiaries of the legacy. Across the leisure facilities and gyms managed by Glasgow Life, equipment will be upgraded under a three year partnership with Technogym, the official fitness equipment supplier to London 2012, ensuring that local communities have access to the latest innovations in fitness.

The refurbishment of the Kevin Hall Indoor Arena, now replaced by the Emirates, is being transformed into a permanent home to bring together physical activity and culture. As well as having a health and fitness centre, a new centre of cultural excellence will bring together 1.5 million items from the city's collections, from Glasgow University's Hunterian Museum and the Scottish Screen Archive. Under a unique partnership between Glasgow Life, Glasgow City Council, the University of Glasgow and the National Library of Scotland, it will see the creation of a Collections Study and Research Centre, Centre for Cultural & Heritage Skills, and a community learning base. With a new digital portal the collections will be brought together online, allowing access globally. £4.5m from the Heritage Lottery Fund was awarded in October 2013 and has helped the project to start in 2015 – this cultural centre will form part of Glasgow's many attractions in the next few years.

Moving on... gaining confidence

Learning from the experience of being host city is important – what could be termed 'strategic learning'. No city authority can go through the process of being host city without emerging changed. If the leadership of Glasgow City Council had known in 2006 when they developed the bid for the Commonwealth Games that there would a global economic crisis and public sector funding pressures on the horizon, it is unlikely that the city would have bid. But by being host city, some of the hardships which accompanied the global crisis have been softened, and the city has weathered the economic downturn better than many others.

Arguably however the main legacy has been the boost in confidence it has received from being host for the Games. The experience has helped leaders across the city to raise their ambitions. Although the City of Culture in 1990 has been viewed as 'successful', by the end of that decade few within the city would have taken seriously the idea of the city hosting a major sporting event – other than in football! The strategy of investing in world class venues – for culture and sport – has paid dividends for the city, and the 2014 Games have been an important step in showing what Glasgow has to offer. With many national and international events coming to Glasgow in the coming years, this success will continue.

The bid for the Youth Olympics Games (YOG) in 2018 was evidence of this emboldened approach. Even though unsuccessful, the Council's confidence in using the bid to speed up regeneration in the north of Glasgow is being seen by residents. The YOG bid also signalled another form of confidence emerging in Glasgow, one built upon connecting with other partners across the country and beyond. The YOG 2018 bid was made in collaboration with the British Olympic Committee and with the Scottish and UK Government. Working in partnerships has been firmly established as the way for the city to continue to invest in facilities and offer new opportunities for its citizens.

This confidence is not restricted to the Council family as the experience of the 2014 Games is likely to reshape the nature of future Commonwealth Games. The successes in Glasgow – the value of having a track record of hosting events, the focus on linking the Games with business as usual, the planning for legacy from the start, the strong relationship between local and national governments, the overwhelming support of people in the city, in Scotland and internationally for the Games, and the cross-party political support are recognised by the CGF and other future potential host cities as valuable components. But the Glasgow approach has also raised challenges to some of the expectations of what future Games need to be. The city has shown that the event need not cost billions of pounds and that investment for the Games can be made with a more explicit link to community use in the future. It has also shown that the formation of an Organising Committee separate from the 'daily business' of the Council may not be the only or ideal model for managing future Games. And it has shown the value of integrating non-sporting events into the programme, enhancing the appeal to people, reinforcing the values of the Games, and showing the contemporary relevance of the Games.

Moving on… building on success

A harder challenge for the city and the Council family will be to maintain the momentum from the Games in different parts of the city. Ensuring that the festival effect and the warm glow of success have a tangible impact on the city has been and will continue to be the focus. Whilst acknowledging that building the legacy will take at least another 5 years, once the spotlight from the Games has been turned off, ensuring that projects and impacts continue to exist will be difficult. To succeed, there will need to be continued political support and financial commitments from both the Scottish Government and Glasgow City Council.

In the East End, the continuing funding and galvanising force of Clyde Gateway led by Ian Manson is vital to ensure that the next phase of the Athletes' Village development continues as planned. The appointment of the chair of the OC, Robert Smith, as the chair of Clyde Gateway is a powerful signal of the desire to ensure that the success of the Games in helping to regenerate the East End of the city will continue. Swift development will be essential to re-build the population base of the area, and allow private sector investment in shops and services. Delays will make it more difficult to capture the public enthusiasm to be part of the regeneration story. Alongside this the Housing Associations allocating the social rented accommodation need to be mindful of the desire of the existing community not to allow gentrification to take place. And for the wider Clyde Gateway project, the challenge is to ensure the public sector investment already committed is able to leverage greater private sector interest and investment into the area. Its ambitious target of £1.5bn private investment over the two decades of its life is important to foster the dynamism required – and to overturn the history of failed momentum for renewal which has blighted the area in the past.

In the north of Glasgow, where local communities have often expressed their concern about being 'left out' from the investment in Commonwealth Games related infrastructure, the transformation of the Sighthill area is a clear legacy from the failed bid to host the Youth Olympics. With funding already committed, the early shoots of renewal are already visible as new lower density social rented housing is being built for Glasgow Housing Association and this needs to be continued through to completion. Significantly as part of the redevelopment, some of the innovative and sustainable building techniques developed for the Athletes' Village are being used to replace the demolished high rise tower blocks.

In a city where change has left many areas of unused and derelict land, imaginative ways will be necessary to help transform them into resources and assets for communities.

The opening of the new Paddlesport centre on the Forth and Clyde canal close to Speir's Wharf in 2014 not only added new life to the former and long derelict power station area, but it did so through working with a charity. And the proposed development of an 'urban park' below the M74 flyover at Port Eglinton by the charity Glasgow Urban Sports has brought together not only the City Council but support from Creative Scotland and Transport Scotland in the design stage.

Moving on... meeting other challenges

Beyond sport and culture, the Games too have helped to leave a legacy. The city's desire to be one of the most sustainable cities in Europe over the next 20 years has the potential to be helped through projects piloted and delivered during the Games. The mass bike hire scheme is due to be expanded in 2015, more dedicated cycle paths created, more district heating systems like that in the Dalmarnock area built. And the innovative techniques in house building and construction used for the Games will become more commonplace across the city. And the City Council's commitment to the environment will be taken forward during the Green Year 2015 celebration of progress, assisted by the new £154m Glasgow Recycling and Renewable Energy Centre (GRREC) at Polmadie, allowing the expansion of the zero waste scheme piloted at the Games venues.

Learning from the Games is also helping the Council to take forward its contribution to the £1.1bn City Deal announced in the autumn of 2014. Financial management and planning developed for the Games capital programme are helping to shape the approach to the enormous investment in infrastructure projects under the City Deal. And governance structures created for the Games are being adapted to help ensure that there is effective partnership working between the 8 local authorities involved in the Glasgow and Clyde Valley project.

And, in turn, these projects and the continuing activity by the Council family are helping to address the deeper and long-term issues which Glasgow faces, especially in relation to health and inequality. With more people in the city involved in sport and physical activity than previously and with modern facilities, with the new schemes helping people furthest from the labour market to get into employment continuing to be supported after the Games, and with a stronger sense of pride in Glasgow, the Games have made an important contribution towards the renewal of the city. But as with all such short lived events, their value lies as much in what people remember of them and the inspiration they get from such memories.

Moving on... but not forgotten

As the Games came to a formal close at Hampden stadium in August 2014, Lord Smith of Kelvin, Robert Smith, the chair of the OC, summed up the sentiment felt by the many people who had contributed to the event and who had been touched in some way by the sport, culture and festivities: "we say farewell to the Commonwealth Games here in Glasgow, but Glasgow will never forget the Games".

And that is what I hope this book will do - help remind us of what worked well and the lessons learnt in the making of the Glasgow Games and ensure that, as the city moves on, the Games will continue to play a part in making and shaping Glasgow's future.

Glasgow's Commonwealth Games, behind the scenes

Glasgow's Commonwealth Games: behind the scenes

Photography Credits

Image: 1, 2, 3, 4, 5, 7, 8, 9, 10, 15, 18, 23, 24, 26, 29, 30, 52, 59, 64, 67, 108, 111, 112, 114, 122, 121

© Abi and Robert Rogerson

Image: 11, 12, 13, 14, 16, 19, 21, 22, 38, 39, 40, 41, 42, 47, 48, 49, 50, 51, 113, 115, 116, 117, 130

© Glasgow Life
© Glasgow City Council

Image: 17, 20, 27, 28, 31, 32, 33, 34, 35, 36, 37, 43, 44, 45, 46, 54, 55, 56, 57, 58, 60, 61, 62, 63, 65, 65, 66, 68, 69, 70, 71, 72, 73, 74, 75, 76, 77, 78, 79, 80, 81, 82, 83, 84, 85, 86, 87, 88, 89, 90, 91, 92, 93, 94, 95, 96, 97, 98, 99, 100, 101, 102, 103, 104, 105, 106, 107, 109, 110, 118, 119, 120, 123, 124, 125, 126, 127, 128, 129, 131, 132, 133, 135, 136, 137, 138, 139

© Newsquest

Image: 25

© Transport Scotland

Image: 6, 53

© Chris Leslie

Image: 134

© Team Scotland

All efforts have been made to gain appropriate permissions for imagery reproduced in this book.